MORE THAN WORDS

MORE THAN
WORDS

Navigating the Complex World of Communication

Natalie Hyde & Valerie Sherrard
Illustrated by David Jardine

   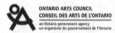

We acknowledge financial support for our publishing activities: the Government of Canada, through the Canada Book Fund and The Canada Council for the Arts; the Government of Ontario, through the Ontario Arts Council, Ontario Creates, and the Ontario Book Publishing Tax Credit. We acknowledge additional funding provided by the Government of Ontario and the Ontario Arts Council to address the adverse effects of the novel coronavirus pandemic.

Library and Archives Canada Cataloguing in Publication

Title: More than words : navigating the complex world of communication /
Valerie Sherrard & Natalie Hyde ; illustrated by David Jardine.
Names: Sherrard, Valerie, author. | Hyde, Natalie, author. |
Jardine, David (Illustrator), illustrator.
Identifiers: Canadiana (print) 20230209874 | Canadiana (ebook) 20230209882 |
ISBN 9781770867192 (hardcover) | ISBN 9781770867208 (HTML)
Subjects: LCSH: Interpersonal communication—Juvenile literature. |
LCSH: Communication—Juvenile literature.
Classification: LCC BF637.C45 S357 2023 | DDC j302.2—dc23

United States Library of Congress Control Number: 2023934902

Cover art: David Jardine
Interior text design: Marijke Friesen
Manufactured by Friesens in Altona, Manitoba in July, 2023.

Printed using paper from a responsible and sustainable resource, including a mix of virgin fibres and recycled materials.

Printed and bound in Canada.

DCB Young Readers
An imprint of Cormorant Books Inc.
260 Ishpadinaa (Spadina) Avenue, Suite 502, Tkaronto (Toronto), ON M5T 2E4
www.dcbyoungreaders.com
www.cormorantbooks.com

For Eliana, who is just learning the power of communication with her first words. — NH

For Matthew and Andrew — superb conversationalists!
— VS aka Grammie

CONTENTS

Introduction

You might be wondering what you're doing holding a book about talking. After all, you already know how to talk. In fact, you've probably been talking since you were a toddler. You don't need to read this.

Or *do* you?

Before you toss this book aside, you should know that there is a whole lot more to this business of communication than you might ever have suspected. In fact, strong communication skills are a lot like a superpower when you know how to use them.

Are you thinking, *Who cares?* Well, actually, lots of people do, and you should too because, just like the bell you can't un-ring, words and actions can never be undone. Most of us can easily think of a time we said or did something we later regretted, all because we didn't communicate wisely.

The good news is that it doesn't have to be that way. You *can* learn to express yourself effectively and avoid the pitfalls that lead to communication fails. This superpower can change your life. Friendships will be stronger! Social activities, better! Your future, brighter!

Say Again?

Communication fails have started wars, sunk ships, destroyed relationships, and – well, the list of disastrous results is pretty much endless. After hitting an iceberg, the communication officer of the RMS *Titanic* sent a bunch of personal messages to friends and family members of passengers *before* he sent a distress signal! It was close to half an hour after the ship hit the iceberg before he finally contacted nearby ships with the Morse code message: "Come at once. Struck a berg." The delay, followed by words that failed to convey the desperate seriousness of the incident, led to responses that were both too little and too late. In fact, the SS *Frankfurt*, which was one of the closest ships, responded, "What is the matter with you?"

This book will help you develop and improve ways to:

✓ recognize and understand nonverbal messages;

✓ avoid common communication pitfalls with your friends and family;

✓ discuss different viewpoints without becoming rude or offensive;

✓ build your critical thinking skills;

✓ learn interesting things about the people in your life;

✓ increase your confidence;

✓ expand how much you know; and

✓ develop greater patience and stronger listening skills.

Besides all that, strong communication skills will make an amazing difference in your professional life. (Okay, you might not have a professional life just yet, but hey, think ahead!)

The chapters follow the normal sequence of a conversation, beginning with a chapter on how to communicate before you say a word, then learning how to genuinely listen to your conversation partner, how to formulate thoughtful and meaningful responses, and even how to end a conversation graciously. There is also a chapter on digital communication, which has its own special challenges in getting your meaning across. Each chapter ends with a recap of the main points and some fun activities to reinforce new skills for both individuals and groups.

Come on in!

The Unspoken

Ask most people what communication means and they'll tell you it's all about what you say and how you say it. And sure, that's important, but it's really only part of the whole picture.

The thing is, we communicate through *way* more than just words. In fact, words alone can be deceptive. A person might say one thing but mean another, and sometimes you can tell what they *really* mean from messages that are unspoken (or nonverbal). For example, have you ever heard someone claim to be fine when their tone, posture, and expression are all telling you the opposite?

That's why understanding basic nonverbal messages is such a big deal, and it's the reason we decided to start with it.

But remember, unless you're talking to yourself, this is always a two-way exchange. Being mindful of *your* signals matters every bit as much! Not being tuned-in to the nonverbal messages you're sending can easily cause a conversation fail!

Learning how to understand those signals from yourself and others is the first superpower in communication. You'll be amazed at how mastering this will up your game!

Let's Begin with Eye Contact

If the thought of looking someone in the eye makes you uncomfortable, you're not alone. This is something a lot of people struggle with. The good news is that overcoming this discomfort *is* possible ... and it's not even complicated. This is one of those times when the dreaded "practice makes perfect" comes in. The more you work at it, the better you become.

One approach you can try is a buddy system. Start with a close friend or family member — someone who's willing to be stared at just for your self-improvement! This person's job will be to offer reminders and track your progress. Since your buddy knows what you're doing, you'll be guaranteed they're making eye contact with *you* too.

But maybe you feel you'd be too self-conscious with the buddy method. If you think that could turn into a two-way awkward-fest, you might find it easier to use mindfulness. In that case, remember to watch for opportunities to make eye contact during any casual conversation.

Try to start a conversation with eye contact, and when you look away, avoid sudden, jerky motions. Also, resist the urge to look at the floor, ceiling, or out the door. That could give the impression that you're planning your escape. Stay focused on the person you're with by shifting your eyes to another part of their face.

Don't Look at Me That Way!

Making eye contact does *not* mean eyeballing someone in a locked-on, bug-eyed, unrelenting stare. That would be creepy. Or it could even feel threatening. Ask any dog. Research shows that they interpret a constant, direct gaze as dominance or aggression.

QUICK
TIP

Use the 50/70 Rule! --
This suggests making eye contact about 50 percent of the time when you're speaking and around 70 percent of the time when you're listening. That might seem like a lot at first, but you can work your way up gradually if you need to. And don't worry, you won't have to set your timer to keep track – just keep those percentages in mind.

Go gently with this newfound skill. Some people have a harder time dealing with direct gazes than others. Eye contact stimulates the layer of the brain that helps people read emotions in faces. For people with autism or post-traumatic stress disorder, too much eye contact can cause overstimulation and result in stress and discomfort.

When you're speaking in a group setting, it's a good idea to make eye contact with one person at a time, finishing a thought or sentence and then moving to someone else. Let your focus move naturally from person to person, not suddenly, as though you're trying to catch someone doing something wrong. And, of course, when someone else is speaking, you should focus on them so that if they look in your direction, they'll see they have your attention.

Still Struggling?

If the thought of looking someone in the eye still makes you anxious, try taking slow, deep breaths before and during the conversation. Breathing from your abdomen (your tummy) can be very relaxing. To learn how to do this, place one hand on the upper part of your chest and the other just below the rib cage. The lower hand is now on top of your diaphragm, which is a muscle that helps us pull air in and push it out again. As you breathe in, make sure your lower hand moves more than your upper hand. This is how you know air is getting right to the bottom of your lungs: the incoming air causes your abdomen to move outward. That's why it is called "abdominal breathing."

This type of breathing also helps prevent the rapid heartbeats that happen when a person is nervous.

Don't be afraid to take small steps. If a few seconds of eye contact is all you can manage to begin with, that is still progress! If you need to, you can even start by looking at a different part of the face, such as a nose or eyebrow. Keep at it and you'll find you can work your way up bit by bit. It's been proven at least a gazillion times that the more you do something, the easier it gets.

QUICK TIP

Practice Eye Contact Online! --------------------------------
There are online videos to let you practice making eye contact. Looking into the eyes of real people who are looking right back at you in a nonthreatening setting may well help you build the confidence you need.

Keep trying. You *will* get there!

But careful! Don't get so caught up in the dos and don'ts of eye contact that you forget to pay attention to the conversation! You're not quite rocking the whole eye contact thing if you have *no idea* what the other person just said.

Is This Really Worth the Bother?

Okay, that all sounds helpful, but you might be wondering, what's the big deal? Does making eye contact *really* matter?

Experts say, "Yes." Not only is it an important part of connecting with others, there are also some pretty significant perks.

Eye contact can make what you say more memorable. *And* it can help the other person remember your face. These benefits are especially helpful when you're meeting new people at school or on vacation, or anywhere you'd like to make a good impression. And let's be honest, not too many of us deliberately set out to make a *bad* impression.

What's more, people are more likely to believe you when you meet their eyes while speaking. (On the other hand, looking down or away can give others the idea that you're being untruthful or that you have something to hide.)

Not only will you come across as believable, but people who meet others' eyes when speaking are generally viewed as more intelligent and confident. The big bonus is that your confidence actually *will* get stronger as you do this, and this in turn will give your natural intelligence a chance to truly shine.

With so many good reasons to make eye contact, it's a communication skill well worth developing.

But guess what. The eyes don't do the job on their own. They're often joined in their expressive efforts by their fuzzy neighbors to the north: namely, the eyebrows.

As partners with the eyes, the eyebrows get in on the act for a wide range of reactions and emotions. They reinforce messages of shock, amusement, doubt, interest, disapproval, astonishment, anger, delight, and many more.

But don't take our word for it! Check yourself out in the mirror looking surprised and disgusted and whatever else strikes your fancy. Notice how your eyebrows raise and lower, arch and scrunch. See how the space between them can widen or narrow depending on the emotion being expressed. Pay attention to the speed and suddenness of their movements.

Your eyebrows are a wealth of information, and they can help identify other facial signals with greater precision.

But Wait! There's a Whole Lot More!

While the eyes and eyebrows are two of the strongest forms of non-verbal communication, there are dozens of other ways we send out messages.

Some of them are easy to interpret, others not so much. But they all have meaning.

Take a moment to picture yourself in the middle of a conversation with someone. Now, imagine that while you're speaking, they suddenly turn around, and you find yourself talking to the back of their head. Or suppose they just get up and walk out of the room, closing the door behind them.

Once you get over being startled, you'd probably think, "Rude!" And you'd be one hundred percent right. That would be an incredibly insensitive way to treat someone who's talking to you.

Fortunately, not many people are *that* rude. Unfortunately, it's not uncommon for people to send other impolite messages during conversations. They're rarely as blatant as the ones just described, but they can still be hurtful. Suppose a friend is sharing a personal story with you. Let's say it happens to be a real tearjerker. What would they think if you looked out the window, picked a bit of lint off your shirt, or sighed? Any of those actions might be done innocently, but your friend could easily take them to mean you aren't interested in what they're saying.

Yes, it's very possible to send out hurtful messages unintentionally. That's why it's important to understand nonverbal communication — not just other people's, but our own as well. Otherwise, you could be "saying" things without intending to.

Every Part Plays a Part --

QUICK
TIP

Every feature on your face can be a treasure trove of information. Don't underestimate the power of your eyes, nose, eyebrows, chin, and mouth.

Those accidental messages can come from different parts of your face. In the middle of it all — the nose!

We don't necessarily think of our noses as particularly useful when it comes to expressing ourselves, but it just so happens they have a few tricks up their, well, their nostrils.

A wrinkled nose could mean you have smelled something distasteful, but it could also signal disapproval. A nose can twitch, sniff, snort, and scrunch, and each of those movements has meaning. Interpreting nosy remarks might be easy, or you might need more information. Luckily, there are usually other clues to help you sniff out the meaning.

And we won't be close-lipped about the mouth!

Our mouths are powerful communicators. Obviously, we use them to speak, but they help us express ourselves in lots of other ways.

With a yawn, for example. Yawns could well be considered the troublemakers of facial expressions. For one thing, seeing someone yawn, and even reading about yawning, can give a person the urge. (It's so contagious, you may even be yawning right now!) People yawn because they're tired, because their body is sending a signal for more oxygen, and, sometimes, because they're bored.

Considering how many triggers there are to make us yawn, you'd think we'd be less likely to jump to conclusions if someone yawns while we're speaking. But instead of giving them the benefit of the doubt, the first thing we think, and sometimes even say, is, "Am I boring you?"

It's not a bad idea, then, to cut others a bit of slack if they happen to yawn while you're speaking. On the other hand, if you find yourself yawning, you might offer a few words to reassure the person you're chatting with that what they're seeing isn't boredom. ("Sorry — I don't know where that came from, but it's definitely not you.")

A smile is a good example of a positive nonverbal message. Fortunately, it's almost as catching as a yawn. (Try it out!) We should all do more smiling! But did you know genuine smiles are expressed by *both* the mouth and the eyes? If a person's mouth is smiling but their eyes are not, their heart might not really be in it.

And not all smiles are friendly and happy. Some of them convey feelings that are spiteful, devious, or vengeful. Others are shy, mysterious, or determined. Learning to recognize whether a smile is genuine isn't as difficult as you might think. Just pay attention to the other nonverbal messages being sent out and put it all together like a pro!

Your mouth can also sneer, quiver, pucker, gape, pout, grimace, part, gasp, purse, tighten, whistle, and sigh. You can bite your upper or lower lip (from the middle or the side), moisten your lips with your tongue, form an O, touch or cover your mouth with your hand or an object, stick your tongue out, clench your teeth, bite a pen or similar object — and the list goes on.

Some of these expressions are easy to read, while others are less so, so it's important to look at the whole picture. This means paying attention to what the rest of the face is saying, of course, but it also includes body language!

What's Your Body Saying?

Let's begin with posture. Maybe that word has you picturing yourself standing straight and tall, shoulders back and chin up. That's great if you're about to march in a parade, but that's not what we're talking about here. In this case, posture simply refers to the way each of us sits or stands under normal circumstances.

Because, yes, something as simple as the way a person sits or stands can be meaningful. However, as you read this section, keep in mind that our bodies aren't always obvious about what they're saying.

Some of the signals a body sends are controlled by the unconscious — we don't realize we're doing them; they just happen naturally. Let's say you're keen to know more about what someone is telling you. If so, you might lean in toward the person speaking. If a conversation isn't to your liking, you're more likely to draw away. Movements like these may be slight and will often occur without you even realizing they're happening.

But of course, there are also conscious movements — movements that we do on purpose and know that we are doing. Hand gestures, for example. They can say a lot, and there are so many of them! While it's true that some cultures tend to employ hand movements more than others, we all use our hands to express many different things. Some are nice, some are not so nice. A thumbs-up, a finger twirling a lock of hair, a chin resting on a fist, the palm of a hand thunking the forehead, fingers spread with tips touching ... this is just a *tiny* sampling of the many hand signals we use every day. No doubt you could come up with dozens more without having to think very hard at all.

Hand Gesture Fail!

Some gestures have different meanings in different cultures. Did you know that the "Okay," "V," and "Thumbs-up" signs are positive in many countries but are considered incredibly rude and offensive in others? Or that the tucked thumb we use to say "I've got your nose" isn't quite so fun to everyone? And crossed fingers don't always imply a wish for good luck.

A palm raised toward someone is generally used to say, "Stop!" or sometimes, "Talk to the hand!" in North America, but it can have a range of different meanings in other parts of the world. And believe it or not, some gestures that are perfectly innocent in many cultures are so offensive in others that they could even lead to your being arrested. Yikes!

While they're less versatile, arms and legs like to have their say too. A seated person whose leg looks like it's trying to dance the jitterbug might be signaling impatience or agitation (or an urge to dance the jitterbug). Arms crossed over the chest could be a sign of an angry, defensive, or critical attitude. But it's just as possible they mean their owner is feeling smug, amused, or maybe just a little chilly.

The way we reach out or touch others is a part of the way we communicate as well. A hug with wide-open arms is probably more heartfelt than one where the elbows remain close to the body (unless you happen to be holding bananas in your armpits). Fingertips gently touching an arm send quite a different message than a finger poking it.

Personal space, also known as proxemics, can significantly affect a person's comfort level during any communication. How close a person is standing, as well as their bearing, can suggest different forms of either affection or aggression. Pay attention to the way your body responds when someone stands especially close to you. You might think nothing of it with a good friend, but your reaction won't be so laid-back if it's a stranger. In that case, you may find your body stiffening. You might lean or even step away; you might notice your breathing and pulse changing. Those are ways your body is warning you of a possible threat when encountering something unfamiliar.

Gauging how much space is enough has a lot to do with how comfortable you feel toward the other person and vice versa. The main thing is to pay attention — to both your reactions *and the other person's.*

QUICK TIP

Screen-to-Screen Chat ------------------------------------
Virtual connections make eye contact impossible and also mean you are unlikely to see some of the body language you would with in-person contact. Pay attention to what you *can* see. Eyes, eyebrows, chin, mouth, head tilts, shoulder shrugs, and not looking at the screen are all clues as to how your virtual conversation is going.

Personal space customs vary from culture to culture. For example, studies tell us that people in South American countries generally need less personal space than people from Asia. Sometimes it depends on relationships, while in other cases it's a general social outlook, with acceptable distance ranging from inches to arm's length.

By now you understand what we meant when we said our bodies aren't always obvious about the messages they're putting out there. That's because the signals they send are often more complex and less universal than many of our facial expressions. This makes it more challenging to be certain of what any one gesture might be telling us. For example, hands thrown in the air might mean delight, excitement, alarm, exasperation, or even surrender.

Well, THAT'S Just Plain Confusing!

It seems like it, doesn't it! But this has all been leading you to an incredibly valuable bit of advice, and one of the most important communication superpowers: *Don't jump to conclusions! Ever!*

Remember how people tend to assume a yawn means boredom, even when it doesn't? Is there a way that mistake could be avoided?

Of course, there is. The yawn couldn't possibly have been the whole story. If the person yawned but had been leaning forward, making eye contact, and reacting in other ways to what was being said, there's no way that was a bored yawn. On the other hand, if their eyes were glazed, their shoulders were slumped, and their toes were tapping on the floor, yep, they were likely bored.

The point is, it's really rare for a person to project a single nonverbal message. Most of the time there will be not one, not two, but a bunch of signals being sent out.

You just need to take it all in. Look at what's going on everywhere — face, hands, posture — and do a little Sherlock Holmes–style figuring. *That's* what's going to make you a certified expert in the art of reading nonverbal communication. (Okay, there might not be a certificate, but really, it's the *skill* that matters.)

When You're Sure! Then What?

Okay, you've read all the signals, and the verdict is in. The person across from you is hanging onto every word you say. You realize you've never been wittier, more charming, or more delightful. You are loved and adored. Yay!

If only it was always that way. Unfortunately, it isn't.

So, what about when there are definitely some negative reactions coming at you? First of all, take a deep breath. Or ten.

Handling negative nonverbal messages is an essential part of successful communication. Each situation is different, and as you expand your skills, you'll get better and better at choosing an effective approach. One vital thing to keep in mind is that everyone sees and expresses things differently.

That means something one person finds highly insulting may seem minor to someone else. Since each of us is unique, this is natural. We interpret and react to nonverbal messages differently, so one of the best tools you can arm yourself with is patience. Don't rush to judgment. Don't shut down in anger. Be ready to give the benefit of the doubt, to clarify, and, most of all, to keep communication channels open. More on that soon.

But First, One Last Thing! (Wait, Isn't That a Contradiction? Anyway ...)

Some nonverbal communication is pretty much universal. In most cultures, you're going to see similar expressions for many emotions: joy, sorrow, fear, anger, surprise, and others. That can make it easier to communicate even when there are language barriers. And that can be a good thing. But don't forget that it can backfire!

Always keep in mind that some gestures you consider friendly could very well be insulting or offensive in other cultures. Remember to look into that before visiting countries where customs could be different!

Hold It! How Are You Going to Remember All This Stuff?

It's a lot, isn't it! You might be thinking you'll never keep it all straight, but over time you'll notice that reading nonverbal communication has become second nature. And that's true for the messages you send *and* the ones you receive!

Remember, now you know a lot about nonverbal communication. That knowledge can be your trusty guide. Use it well!

Chapter One Activities

Individual Activities

Mirror Mime

This is best if done in front of a full-length mirror so that you can see all of your body movements. See how well you're able to convey each emotion listed below, first using body language *and* facial expressions, and then body language only. Pay particular attention to the ways you move your hands, feet, shoulders, head, and so on when you *do* and then when you *don't* use facial expressions.

- ✓ Surprise
- ✓ Affection
- ✓ Anger
- ✓ Excitement
- ✓ Boredom
- ✓ Doubt
- ✓ Anxiety
- ✓ Sympathy
- ✓ Shock

The Drama!

Choose a show that you can record or is available to watch a second time, one where you know the acting is likely to be a little (or a lot) overdone. Soap operas and sitcoms can be good choices for this. Turn off the sound so you can watch either a segment or the whole episode without hearing the dialogue. (No closed captions either!) Watch the nonverbal messages closely — the expressions on faces, the gestures, movements, and other aspects of body language. What do you think is happening? Can you guess at the storyline enough to figure out where there's conflict, confusion, deception, and more? A second viewing with the sound on will tell you how close you came!

Group Activities

I'm Offended!

It's possible to offend, hurt, or annoy others with our body language without even realizing we're doing it. The more we know about ways our actions can be interpreted, the easier it will be to avoid that kind of communication fail!

As a group, list all of the gestures, expressions, and types of body language that could be considered negative (keep it PG, people!). Then each person should choose what they see as the two most offensive and two least offensive items from the list. Discuss why individuals made the selections they did. Being aware of how different people are affected by various nonverbal messages will help you develop greater sensitivity to others.

That's Handy!

How many hand signals can you think of? Start with a two-minute time limit. Each member of the group writes down as many words or phrases expressed by hand (or hand and arm) signals as they can in those two minutes. When finished, each person reads their list. The others respond by showing what they believe to be the hand signal that expresses each item. It will be interesting to see how many are easily recognized and demonstrated correctly by most or all of the group members. Some lesser-known signals may be useful for the others to learn.

Chapter One Rapid Recap

✓ There are loads of ways to send and receive information without saying a word. These include facial expressions, body language, and more.

✓ It's a two-way street. Always pay attention to your own nonverbal messages as well as those coming from the people you're communicating with.

✓ Nonverbal messages can either support or contradict what a person says.

✓ Making eye contact shows your interest in what the other person is saying and has many other benefits.

✓ Universal nonverbal messages can be helpful when there are language barriers, but be aware some have different meanings in other cultures.

CHAPTER TWO

Totally Terrific Tip-Top Talking Tips

Did you notice the title of the chapter? Since this one is about talking, we thought it might be fun to start with a bit of a tongue twister. Try saying it out loud quickly five times in a row. Not easy, is it?

In fact, when it comes to talking, there are lots of things that aren't as easy as we might expect. Saying the wrong thing, or even the right thing in the wrong way, can lead to trouble — and nobody needs that! *You* know what you mean when you say something, but that doesn't guarantee everyone else will. If your intended message ends up confusing, misleading, or even offending, you won't be doing any communication fist bumps to celebrate.

Words Worth --
What you say is more important than you might realize. Have you ever considered that words are the main building blocks in your relationships?

In one sense, words represent you to the world. They aren't the only things that do, of course, but they count for a lot. They carry thoughts and ideas, questions and answers, memories, hopes, dreams, and so many other things that make up the person that is uniquely you.

Naturally, this is a two-way street. Your opinions and feelings about others are formed, at least in part, by their words. If you pause to think about some of the people in your life, you can almost certainly remember things they've said over the years.

Some of those memories are great, aren't they? Words of encouragement, comfort, and even laughter. Happy memories are often wrapped around things that were said. On the other hand, cutting, hurtful, or angry words also remain with us. We hear them both — the positive and the negative — long after they were spoken.

Words are also the foundation for growth and learning as we make our way through life. We rely on them more than you might ever have realized. You'll know how true that is if you've ever tried to explain something to someone when you don't speak each other's language. Getting a message across is difficult, to say the least! Wild gestures only go so far.

But even when we do speak the same language, there are challenges that can get in the way. Let's take a closer look at the different parts of communication.

Beginning with Words

The words you use when you're speaking have a huge impact on how you come across. If that sounds totally obvious, we'd like you to think about why we've mentioned it. Consider this: you almost certainly talk differently around your friends than you do when you're having a conversation with your parents, teachers, or older relatives. It's natural for all of us to adapt the words we use to the circumstances and people we're with at any given time.

Recognizing that there are places and situations that call for a bit of good behavior means you already know this part is important. The question is: *Do you have all the skills you need to adjust your speaking habits when it really matters?* You may find it easy to be more mannerly or respectful when it's called for, but what about some of the other things that affect the impression you give?

What about — yes, we're going to use the dreaded G-word — what about ...

Grammar

You might not think grammar is important. Or interesting. And both of those things might be true for you — today. But is that always going to be true?

Maybe you can answer that by doing a little imaginary time traveling. How about sending yourself a few years into the future? We're betting you can picture more than one situation where Future You will be glad to know some of the language rules that don't matter to you right now.

Perhaps you're thinking, *But those rules are hard, and there are so many of them!*

It's true there are quite a few rules about grammar, but the basic things you need to know really aren't that overwhelming or difficult. As is the case for anything else that's worthwhile, a small investment of time and effort will make a big difference. The more you practice good grammar, the more natural it will feel to you.

Come On! Does Anybody Seriously Care about Grammar Anymore?

You'd be surprised. While most people aren't impolite enough to point out grammatical errors, there are plenty of folks who *notice* those slips.

QUICK TIP

Find It Online! -- Search "Basic Rules of Grammar" and "Common Grammar Mistakes." Master one or two facts at a time. Before you know it, you'll feel confident enough to speak up in most settings.

Grammar is about consistent, correct use of language. It's also about clarity. The stronger your grammar skills are, the easier it will be for people to understand what you're saying. You'll sound smarter and more educated. And you might even have a positive influence on the way people around you speak. Just be careful not to be pushy about it. People rarely appreciate being corrected. Lead by example, not lectures!

Here are just a few times and places where you'll feel more confident and comfortable if you know you're expressing yourself using basic grammar rules:

✓ At school — at any level.

✓ On social media. (Mistakes in written comments can really stand out!)

✓ Whenever you're meeting new people.

✓ At family and community gatherings.

✓ Shopping, eating out, or going anywhere else where you'd interact with strangers.

✓ At places of worship.

✓ And, let's face it, we don't know what might apply to you, so we challenge you to add a few things to this list based on your personal circumstances.

Also, let's not forget Future You, who will welcome good grammar in numerous work and social situations!

Using Meaningful Language

First, let's talk about what's at our disposal. Just how many words do you think there are in the English language?

Pause here to think about it. Make it a dramatic pause, if possible, because that's so much more suspenseful!

The answer is —

Wait! Before we reveal that number, let's talk about the average vocabulary. A vocabulary is all the words you know, but we can separate those words into two categories: the active, or words you use regularly, and the passive, which are words you recognize and understand but don't often use.

The average English speaker's vocabulary consists of 20,000 active and 40,000 passive words.

And now, the exciting reveal! How many words are there in the English language? Would you believe 750,000! That's right! One of the biggest dictionaries includes three-quarters of a million words, all available for you to use.

That's not to say you should be learning and using all of them. Lots of words are only used by people in specific types of work. If you're not a marine biologist, you may never find yourself discussing *Ittibittium*. And if you're not a doctor, you won't be diagnosing any cases of pneumonoultramicroscopicsilicovolcanoconiosis.

The 20,000 to 40,000 words you most likely know are plenty for your everyday use.

But let's face it — it's easy to get lazy with our vocabulary. Instead of searching for a word with genuine meaning, we sometimes toss out a tired, overused one.

For example: "This painting is awesome."

That remark tells us the speaker likes the painting, and nothing else. We don't know why. We don't know what it was about the painting that drew the remark. Is it mysterious, captivating, majestic, stunning, haunting, tranquil, dazzling, charming — we could go on, but you get the idea. Does it change your mood or how you feel? What thoughts might there be about the texture, the sense of movement, the ways in which color was used?

Which brings us to these questions: *Why use meaningless, overused words when you express yourself? Why not get in the habit of using words that truly say what you want to convey?*

This takes time and practice, but it's really not difficult. And the result is so pleasing! People will enjoy listening to you speak because you'll sound more interesting and intelligent. Which you are!

Here are some guidelines and tips to polish your prose:

1. Think about what you want to say. That might seem obvious, but the "lazy" words are usually in those first thoughts. Learn to recognize them and replace them with words that carry more depth and meaning.

2. Make regular use of a thesaurus. This will help your vocabulary grow so the right words will be there when you need them.

3. Check the correct application when it comes to new words. Not everything the thesaurus suggests will be right for specific uses.

4. Get in the habit of eliminating meaningless words. You'll learn to recognize them easily when you start considering the meanings of the words you're using.

5. Try to avoid saying "um," "like," "uh," and so forth. Those "pause fillers" can make it sound like you're unsure of what you want to say.

6. Don't be afraid to inject greater emotion and emphasis when you're speaking.

Before you know it, you'll be expressing yourself eloquently and with precision!

More than Words

As we've just discussed, what you say matters, but it doesn't begin and end there. Just as important as *what* you say is *how* you say it. Every time you speak, your words are carried by a team of assistants, and each of them is doing their part to get your full meaning across.

This is a good thing most of the time. When the team members are working in sync with what you mean to say, your message will be stronger and clearer. On the other hand, if one of them slips up, the results can be awkward.

Let's look at some of these assistants and what happens when they malfunction.

Focus and Clarity

Have you ever listened to someone jabber on and on about something until whatever they are trying to say has been buried under a perplexing pile of words? Have you ever found *yourself* doing it? It's not exactly an effective way to communicate.

Oddly enough, it's often when we care deeply about a subject or are determined to prove or disprove something that our words will speed up, race off in all directions, and leave our audience lost and confused.

Something similar can happen, although at a less frantic pace, when you wander off topic because other thoughts pop into your head while you're talking. Allowing yourself to get distracted and segue into detours makes it very difficult for the person you're speaking with to follow along. Sometimes your conversation can get so convoluted you end up tripping over your own tongue!

So how can you avoid making that particular communication mistake?

The fact is, this isn't a quick and easy thing to fix. It takes effort and focus, but the result can be *amazing*. Here are some tips for keeping you on track to get your message across:

1. First of all, be sure you know your subject well enough to share it with others. Ditto if you're telling a story. It's rarely enjoyable for the listener to have someone recounting an event when they're shaky on the details or, worse, can't remember the ending.

2. Keep the story or information you're sharing as a firmly fixed point in your mind. Learn to recognize those tempting side thoughts as disruptions — that story about your cat may be worth telling at some point, but not just now! Having your thoughts organized will help you stay on topic.

3. As much as possible, get rid of distractions around you. Turn off or mute electronics and find a space where other nearby activities won't grab your attention (or your audience's)!

4. If you find your concentration slipping, inviting input from the other person can help you refocus and possibly even gain clarity.

Once you've mastered the art of staying on topic, you'll notice your confidence and your ability to express yourself improving by leaps and bounds. And you know who else will notice those things? The people you're talking to!

Your words will gain credibility and strength, and those are qualities that make others listen. Not only will people pay closer attention, they'll find it so much easier to grasp what you're saying, which is, after all, pretty much the whole point of communication.

The Sound of Your Voice

The phone rings! You answer (usually a good strategy). "Hello," you say.

"Hi," responds the person on the other end of the line.

And from that single, short word, you know who it is.

That's how distinctive our voices are. Even with all the people in your life, you can probably identify many of them just by hearing them speak a word or two.

They recognize your voice too, of course. But you know who might have trouble with that? You! The first time you heard yourself in a recording, you probably thought, *Wait! I don't sound like that — do I?* There's an explanation for why that happens.

When you're speaking, the sound of your voice is being transmitted to you from both outside and inside. That creates a depth and resonance that only you hear. Played back on a recording, however, when the sound is transmitted only from the outside, what you hear typically sounds higher and less rich. That's how you sound to other people.

One of the amazing things about the human voice is the range of sounds it's capable of making. You can convey so much with the melody or emotion in your voice.

It's natural for your tone and pitch to rise and fall when you speak. This helps convey what you're feeling, whether you're happy, sad, angry, amused, frightened, triumphant, panicked, scared, menacing ... the list is as endless as human emotion.

Besides the expressions in our speech, we also use our voices to sing, scream, shout, laugh, and more. All of those things are expressed not only through words but by the timbre and tone, the

"He's never late for anything."

"I just adore homework."

"Please don't offer me
another cookie."

"Oh, no — these books
aren't heavy."

pitch and volume produced by the vocal cords. When you think about all they can do, they're really quite astonishing!

Consider this! You can actually say something in such a way that the listener will understand your meaning is the *exact opposite* of your words!

Try it out! Help these four teens get their messages across by lending them your voice and reading their remarks in a way that contradicts the words themselves.

Most of us are accustomed to this tongue-in-cheek way of expressing something and have no trouble recognizing when someone's meaning is at odds with their words. But what about folks who take such remarks literally? They may be puzzled, or perhaps even embarrassed, like someone left on the outside of a private joke. Be sensitive to others when using this technique and be ready to clear up their confusion with a discreet explanation.

Monotone is a word we use to describe a voice when all the words are expressed at the same level. This can make it challenging to read between the lines. That's because when someone speaks in a monotone, the ups and downs we hear in more expressive speech aren't present. If you tend to speak this way, you can practice adding feeling to your words to strengthen your communication. And if you're talking to someone who speaks in a monotone, listen carefully and ask for clarification if you need to.

Inflection fail! *Heavy sarcasm*! One thing that can really send a conversation off the rails is sarcasm, a common weapon used when someone is angry or insecure. While it likes to pass itself off as a joke, sarcasm is one form of humor that can cause real hurt. When sarcasm shows up, it's always linked arm in arm with mockery and contempt. It can't hide its mean streak, and it leaves a trail of awkwardness and embarrassment in its wake. Don't use it. You're nicer than that.

Volume

Have you ever witnessed a scene where a group of people keep raising their voices, trying to make themselves heard over one another? The result is what we call a din. Otherwise known as noise — which sometimes means no one can hear what anyone else is saying!

Remember how ineffective that strategy is when *you* get the urge to speak over others. All that does is raise the level of the whole conversation. Instead, wait for a break and then go ahead.

Of course, not every occasion for speaking loudly is a contest to be heard, and there are times when you'll want your voice to carry a sense of authority or leadership. As long as you're careful to keep from sounding aggressive or pushy, you'll be fine.

When You Need to Turn Down the Volume ------------------
Being aware is the main thing, but it may also help to breathe deeply from your diaphragm, which can help soften and lower your voice.

Some professionals have found that speaking quietly can actually be more powerful than speaking loudly. A soft voice forces the audience to be quiet and listen carefully. They're likely to pick up on what the speaker emphasizes and to better retain what they've heard because their attention was so fully engaged.

What's the Hurry?

Have you ever heard someone talking so fast it almost sounds as though their sentences are one incredibly looooooooong and jumbled word? Not only is it difficult to sort out what a speed-talker is saying, it's also hard to process their words or form a response because they barely finish one sentence before rushing on to the next.

There are several reasons why people talk at a rapid rate. For example, they may be anxious, it may be a lifelong habit, or it could be they're trying to express thoughts and ideas before they forget them. Whatever the cause, it can prevent effective communication. It also tends to make the speaker sound out of breath and a little frantic.

Normal talking speed is about 125 words per minute. Now you might be thinking, *Hey, I wonder how many words a minute I average when I'm talking?* Well, here's a tip. Don't try to count them while you're talking. That's really hard, and it tends to make a person blurt out numbers in the middle of a conversation. If you really want to check that out, simply record yourself during a normal conversation and use a timer to help you get your word count afterward.

If *you're* a speed-talker, there are things you can do about it. The first is the most important: *Be aware.* If you're consciously monitoring your speech and making a genuine effort to pace yourself, your own awareness will be a huge help. As you do this, try to form a habit of taking a full breath when you pause for air. This helps you set a more relaxed pace and prevents the need to rush through your words before you run out of oxygen.

You may also ask others to remind you to slow down when necessary, or use a prop, such as a glass of water to sip from, to create breaks in your conversation.

Warning! Be aware that there are times when talking rapidly is deliberate and may involve ill intentions. So pay careful attention when you encounter a speed-talker who's trying to persuade you about something. They may be speeding along because they don't want to give you time to form thoughts that challenge or contradict what they're saying. Often, you can tell this is happening because you feel pressured or uneasy. In that case, the best strategy is to say you need to think it over. Don't agree to anything right then and there no matter how persuasive they try to be.

To Blurt or Not to Blurt

You might be surprised to know that blurting isn't *always* a bad thing to do. When someone's about to touch something hot, for example. That's not the time to pause and carefully consider the best way to warn them. In those cases, go ahead and blurt out, "No!" or "Stop!" or whatever other warning pops into your head, and do it just as quickly as you can.

Those moments are exceptions, though. Under normal circumstances, it's a good idea to follow the old adage, "Think before you speak." How many times have you found yourself embarrassed or horrified over something you've blurted out? It's happened to most of us, but it's possible to avoid such gaffes by pausing for a second or two. That's usually enough time to keep you from making a remark you'll end up hearing over and over in your head for pretty much the rest of your life.

Speaking with care — taking those seconds to measure and consider your words — has other benefits as well. For one thing, it helps you to relax, to breathe properly, and to feel in control.

The Pause

Yes, a pause is part of conversation. It's a part with no words, but it still qualifies as a part of speech. In fact, a pause, used well, can be an incredibly powerful tool. That's why we'd like to pause to tell you what a well-placed pause can do:

- It gives you two or three seconds to collect your thoughts and make sure you're staying on track.
- It gives you a chance for a good, deep breath, which can also be calming.
- It holds your audience's attention, and it can even get it back when there are signs their focus is drifting.

Learning to use the pause when you're speaking is one more way to improve your communication, so *do* hesitate to use it!

Keeping It Real

If you ask two people to write out a conversation they just had, they'd probably find it difficult to remember exactly what was said and in what order. Each person's account might be different, sometimes in small and sometimes in significant ways.

Ask those people to recreate the same conversation a week or a month later and it's unlikely they'd be able to recall much of it with any accuracy.

But there's one aspect of the conversation that could very well remain consistent in memory. What was said will fade, but how they *felt* may endure. Emotional reactions stay with us, which is why you may remember feeling joyous, amused, angry, sad, or any range of emotions long after the words that were spoken have gone from memory.

Does this matter? It does indeed, and very much. Emotions are the cornerstone of relationships. The most important thing you can do to grow meaningful connections is simply to be genuine in your communications.

A Silent World

Think about it! Imagine a world with no words. What do you think it would look like? Consider that pretty much everything that's ever been invented has depended on complex thought. And complex thought cannot be fully expressed or shared without words. Might a wordless world take us all back to a Stone Age type of existence?

So, ramp up that vocabulary, keep in mind your tone, inflection, volume, and grammar, and put power into your speech.

Chapter Two Activities

Individual Activities

The Sound of Myself

Record yourself reading a passage from a favorite book. Choose something with elements such as action, emotion, tension, humor — just as long as it grabs your interest. When you've finished, play it back. Does your voice bring the story to life? Would it be better if your pace or volume were different? Can you hear how the story makes you feel in the way you read it? Repeat until you're happy with the results. Try this again with different stories and passages. It will create awareness that will help your speaking skills grow and improve.

What's in a Word?

Learn how to add meaning and emotion to individual words by using rising and falling tones, emphasis, and timbre. This is called inflection or intonation. See how saying the words "Always," "Never," and "Sometimes" just with different inflections can shift their meaning.

Inflection	Always	Never	Sometimes
Rising			
Falling			
Neutral			
Doubtful			
Certain			
Bored			
Excited			
Surprised			
Disinterested			
Insistent			
Enthusiastic			
Commanding			
Compliant			

Group Activities

Filler Quest

What are fillers? They're the words we use when we pause to focus or decide what to say next. Fillers are a crutch, and recognizing how often we rely on them is an important step toward eliminating them from our conversation.

In this game, we'll concentrate on three of the most common fillers: *um*, *uh*, and *like*. (Note that *like* only applies when it is used as described above, and not when it is an appropriate part of a sentence.)

Each person is to draw a slip of paper with a topic on it, and they must talk about that subject for one minute. Those listening are to raise a hand every time they hear a filler word being used. After three filler words, the speaker is out, and play moves to the next person in line to speak.

Any player who manages to get to the end of their minute without using a filler word may be awarded a prize or given a round of applause.

Filler Quest Sample Topics (feel free to add your own)				
Education	Hobbies	Last book read	Bucket list	Best dessert
Favorite song	Siblings	Prize possession	Favorite TV show	Fashion
Last holiday	Fears	Inventions	Sports	Early memory
Best pet	Career plans	Music	Pet peeve	My room
Bad habits	Best lunch	Video games	Seasons	Social media

Analyze This!

Using meaningful, descriptive words is a great way to enhance your speaking skills, whether you're telling a story, describing something, or answering a question. This activity will help reinforce the importance of carefully choosing the words you use.

1. Divide players into Team A and Team B. Each team must prepare slips of paper with ten or more subjects for the other team to draw from. Subjects should be common objects or living creatures.

2. Team A chooses one person as the analyst and sends them out of the room while the team draws a subject from the slips prepared by Team B.

3. When the analyst returns, Team A members take turns describing the subject, giving *one clue at a time*. (For example, if the object is an elephant, clues could be: gigantic, gray, big ears, trunk, and so on.)

4. Each clue given adds one demerit point to the team's score. The analyst stops play when ready to guess the subject. If the guess is correct, the round ends.

5. If the guess is incorrect, an additional demerit point is given as a penalty, and play resumes. Play ends when a maximum of ten clues have been given. If the analyst is still unable to correctly identify the subject, two additional demerit points are added, and the round ends.

6. It is now Team B's turn to select an analyst and follow the same procedure. When both teams have played an equal number of rounds, all points are added, and the team with the *lowest* score is declared the winner.

Chapter Two Rapid Recap

✓ Improve your vocabulary by using more expressive, specific words.

✓ Get acquainted with good grammar — you'll be glad you did.

✓ Keep focused on the topic when you speak.

✓ Use a pause to gather your thoughts or regain attention.

✓ Put emotion into your speech with inflection and intonation.

✓ Remember, things cannot be unsaid once they are heard, so be aware of the messages you are sending.

-CHAPTER THREE-

Listen Up!

Chapter Two was all about expressing ourselves. It examined various ways we can do that with clarity and depth. That's a great start, but it's only one side of a conversation, and we all know conversation isn't one-sided — not even when we're talking to ourselves!

For communication to be meaningful, a number of important skills are needed. And that brings us to the next component.

Listening

Pause for one moment to think about someone you know who listens when you're talking to them. *Really* listens, in a way that tells you they're truly paying attention to you. It feels good, doesn't it?

Now think of people who interrupt, let their attention wander, or look like they can hardly wait for you to finish talking so they can speak. That doesn't feel so great.

In the second scenario, you don't feel genuinely heard, and for a good reason! The person you were talking to was barely listening. They heard some of what you said, but not in a meaningful way. Not in a way that told you what you were saying mattered.

Listening well isn't a skill many of us were born with. Most of us have to work at it, but is it ever worth the effort. When you develop good listening skills, everybody benefits. In fact, every good conversationalist knows that listening is just as important as speaking. Let's explore how and why that is.

QUICK TIP

Are You Listening? --
Show someone you're actually listening to them by paying attention, making eye contact, and not interrupting. When they are done speaking, summarize what they said without being dismissive.

Listening and Hearing: Aren't They the Same Thing?

Nope. If that surprises you, consider this: we live in a noisy world. There are sounds around us nearly all the time. But our auditory senses have been trained to ignore background racket so that they can focus on a particular sound. That's why you can hear a single voice even in a room where there's noisy chatter and music playing. We also tend to tune out some of the things we hear in our daily routine. When we think it's silent, the air may actually be alive with sounds like trees rustling, appliance motors humming, and more. We just don't notice.

That's because *hearing* is a passive act — something that happens without any effort on our part. Sounds float around us; some of them get our attention, others don't. Much of the time, we're only listening at about a quarter of our actual capacity. That, sadly enough, is even true when it comes to what we hear when other people are speaking.

You see, there's another big reason we don't register more of what we hear, and, to be perfectly frank, it's a little embarrassing. The fact is, many of us are a whole lot more interested in talking about ourselves or offering our opinions than we are in hearing what others have to say. We may even *interrupt* to talk about our own experiences or to make suggestions before the other person has finished speaking.

RUDE!

Not only is that bad manners, it can actually prevent learning! After all, if what you hear the most is your own voice talking about things you already know, there's not much opportunity for new information to get in.

QUICK
TIP

Stop and Listen --
Make a mental note to check out your reaction the next time you hear a sound you can't identify. Chances are, you'll stop and listen carefully as you try to figure out what it is. That's an example of first *hearing* something and then *listening* for the source.

Listening, on the other hand, is deliberate and purposeful. When you listen, you're paying attention. Listening is *active*: it doesn't happen on its own, and there's a lot more to it than you might imagine. Developing top-notch listening skills is a vital part of your new superpower, so get ready to try out some of our tips!

The first thing to keep in mind is that active listening doesn't come naturally to most of us. We need to work at it. And before we work at anything, we usually like to know it matters. It does, and here are a few reasons why.

Listening leads to meaningful connections. As we mentioned earlier, good listeners are very much appreciated. Family, friends, and others in your life will value the way you pay attention to them, just as you do when others truly listen to you. They'll feel heard and supported, which will benefit your relationships and make you someone others enjoy talking with.

✓ **Listening shows respect for the speaker.** This may seem obvious, but the ripple effect can be surprising. Your respectful attention will tell others you're intelligent, trustworthy, and caring. And it puts you in a good position to provide emotional support.

✓ **Listening develops your processing and problem-solving skills.** When you listen thoughtfully, you'll absorb what you hear in a deeper way. Reflecting on what you've heard will allow you to respond with pertinent questions and observations. And of course, the more you use your brain analytically, the better you'll be at working out solutions.

So now you know! Active listening comes with big benefits. All you have to do is put in the effort to master one part at a time, which you can do because you're a person with determination!

But perhaps you're doubting us! Maybe you're thinking, *Come on, how complicated can it be? All you have to do is plain old* listen, *right?*

How about if we lay it all out and let you decide that for yourself?

Mastering the "Simple" Art of Active Listening

Here are the steps you'll want to take on your path to becoming a listening pro:

1. **Be sure the other person knows you're engaged.** Use nonverbal communication to show your interest. You can achieve this by:
    a. making regular eye contact;
    b. nodding;
    c. leaning in; and
    d. reacting appropriately with a smile, frown, raised eyebrow, and so on.

2. **Pay attention not just to *what* they're saying but *how* they're saying it.** Their tone and manner of expression as well as their facial and body language messages will allow you to more fully understand the message in their words.

3. **Play it back.** You can clarify what's being said by repeating it in your own words. This also allows any misunderstanding to be cleared up. You can do this by starting with phrases like:
    a. So what you're saying is ...
    b. It sounds like ...
    c. If I understood this point ...
    d. In other words ...

4. **Do not interrupt!** Not to answer, not even to ask a question. Remind yourself that you haven't heard them out yet, and you won't really know how to respond until they've finished speaking. It's good manners, and it can help you avoid embarrassment, which happens so easily when we interrupt before we hear the whole story.

5. **Never try to talk over someone — not even if they've interrupted you!** You already know that can lead to chaos, and if someone butts in when you're speaking, they clearly don't have the kind of listening skills you're using. No good can come from raising your voice to try to override the other person in those situations. Let them speak and then politely ask them to allow you to finish making your point before you go on.

6. **Be sure you're getting it right.** Ask questions. Take time to process the details of what you're hearing. Don't make assumptions; when you need to, double-check. Request evidence to verify what they're saying if necessary. (And use critical thinking — which we'll talk about in the next chapter.)

7. **Turn off preconceptions so that you can properly consider what you're hearing.** If you've already decided you agree or disagree, your brain will start churning out imaginary thumbs-up or thumbs-down emojis, and your active listening will grind to a halt. Do your best to listen from a neutral position.

8. **Stay focused on the message.** Most discussions are two-way streets, where you're each sharing thoughts and opinions. But there's always a danger of someone wandering off on a tangent, and that can confuse the matter. If you see that happening, do your best to politely steer the conversation back to the original topic.

9. **Process with care.** It's not enough to pay attention to words or sounds. You need to consider them too. Make sure you've processed all information fully. This helps you avoid making assumptions and allows you to respond appropriately, which is an important part of strong communication.

10. **Be empathetic.** Whoa! This is a *big* one. We'd better give it its own section.

Empathy: Who Cares?

You do, if you're empathetic. Empathy is being able to understand and share what someone else is feeling. It's different from sympathy or pity. Empathy allows you to not only recognize but *experience* how another person is feeling.

There are three parts to empathy.

First, there's the thinking part, when you take in information. For example, hearing that your friend's dog died is a factual statement. Life has cycles, and death is a natural part of that. It's a detail you could potentially understand on a cold, clinical level.

Except, most of us don't. In the second part of empathy, there is an immediate response. That response — a visceral response — is one of feeling. It's when you relate on an emotional level. You may remember a time when you felt loss and grief, and those emotions will surface in relation to your friend's loss. As this happens, you will experience some degree of the sadness your friend is experiencing.

The last part of empathy is compassion. This goes beyond relating to what your friend is feeling. Compassion is when you say or do something comforting to help your friend feel better or just let them know you support them.

Empathy helps you connect with others in a deep and meaningful way. It shows that you understand, genuinely care, and desire to console or encourage them.

Not Sure You're the Empathetic Type?

Empathy doesn't come naturally to everyone. But if it's something you want to master, it can be learned. As with so many things in life, all you need is the will to do it and some practice.

One thing to keep in mind is that it's a lot easier to be empathetic with someone you know well. If a stranger on the bus told you their dog just died, your emotional reaction wouldn't be the same as it would be if you heard the same thing from a close friend. Even so, you would recognize that the stranger is hurting, and you can still express caring.

That's because loss and grief are universal human experiences. There are very few of us who haven't felt sad, although the details and depth of our sadness will depend on the circumstances. There are almost always events in your own life that you can draw on to help you understand someone else's feelings.

It's also important to remember that the degree to which a person feels any type of emotional pain is based on many things, so it's a good idea not to judge or assume someone is overreacting or perhaps looking for attention, just because their response to a situation is greater than yours would be.

Suppose, for example, you see a child sobbing inconsolably over a broken toy. You might think they are overdoing it. It's just a toy — something that can be replaced. And they probably have lots more at home. Your first impulse may be to make light of it and possibly say something unsympathetic.

But what if that toy was the last thing a grandparent ever gave to the child? Or what if it was something they had spent a long time saving up for in order to buy it on their own? Would knowing either of those details change your reaction?

Thinking Shortcut

To be truly empathetic, we need to set aside our biases. Biases are when we favor one thing – such as a person, a thing, or an idea – over all others. Often, we're not even conscious of our biases. Biases can keep us from thinking something through thoroughly. That can lead us to reaching the wrong conclusions or making poor decisions. Even when we think we know the whole picture, there are often things we're not aware of.

Developing more empathy takes effort, but it's worth it. It will build and strengthen your ability to relate to and respond to others. Your ability to show empathy will play a huge role in the strength of your relationships with friends, family, and even people you work for and with later in your life.

The Empathy Shop

Maybe you've realized you're not exactly the empathetic type, but you'd like to change that because you can see it would make a grand addition to your communication superpowers. And you're right about that!

Unfortunately, you can't dash down to the local store or go online and order a supply. Empathy is something that has to be nurtured and grown. Here are a couple of suggestions to help you get started:

1. **Expand your human horizons!** Spend time researching other people's cultures: the hardships they've overcome, injustices they've faced, kindnesses they've encountered. Past experiences inform and shape all of our lives. The more you know about other cultures and their history, the better you can relate to them. There are plenty of ways you can get familiar with backgrounds that are different from your own. Besides general research methods, you can learn a great deal by connecting one-on-one with individuals and listening with an open mind. You can also put yourself in places where you'll broaden your exposure to all kinds of other experiences. This can be as varied as traveling to other places or just taking a different

route in your daily routine. You might try new foods, explore new social settings, or get involved with groups and activities you haven't considered before. There are so many interesting and wonderful people out there — enrich your life and increase your empathetic skills by getting to know more of them!

Let Me Help with That! --
Volunteering is a great way to build empathy. You can volunteer at a food pantry, visit a nursing home, clean up in your community, or help deliver meals. Seeing how other people live and deal with struggles is a first step in building empathy.

QUICK TIP

2. **Put it on hold!** It's often tempting, when someone is sharing a problem, to jump in with a solution. And sure, solutions can be good, but providing one is not always the best course of action. The person with the problem may already know what to do. After all, if you thought of a solution while they were still talking, chances are it's occurred to them too. In some situations, what they need more than a pat answer is someone to listen and provide emotional support. Give them a chance to share their feelings and then gently bring the conversation around to your answer after they've felt heard and cared about.

3. **Hurry up and wait.** As with offering quick solutions, it's easy to interrupt when someone is sharing a painful story. We looked at that bad habit earlier, but one thing we didn't mention was that this can prevent the development of empathy. How? It not only stops you from hearing the whole story from the other person, it also keeps you from forming a truly empathetic response: thinking, feeling, caring!

4. **Recognize when your own opinions and biases are getting in the way.** Remember earlier when we talked about your friend's dog dying? What if you really, really, really didn't like dogs? That might make it difficult for you to relate to their sadness. Learning to recognize when you're reacting on the basis of your own feelings will allow you to take a step back, consider the situation objectively, and find an emotional bridge. As long as you understand what your friend is feeling (loss, grief), you can look past the part you don't quite get and relate what they're feeling to a comparable experience of your own.

Whew! That was a lot of information about what looked like a simple subject, wasn't it? Except, we're not actually finished yet! You won't be fully equipped with the listening part of your communication superpower until you know how to sidestep the pitfalls!

Things That Get in the Way of Listening

We hope you're convinced of the benefits of being a good listener. And don't be hard on yourself if you haven't nailed it by the end of the week! Even those who use good listening skills struggle with it at times, and there are a few things that make that struggle hard:

1. **Sight and sound distractions.** It's difficult to listen well when there are sounds and activities nearby. Some disturbances can be dealt with, but there are others you have no control over. A television can be turned off, but a marching band of drum-banging chimpanzees is quite another matter. When you can't eliminate a distraction, you may be able to change locations,

or pause if it's something you can wait out. If none of those options are possible, you may have to shift your concentration into overdrive and do your best to focus in spite of the distraction.

2. **Physical distractions.** Have you ever been chatting on the phone and realized you're overdue for a pit stop? Yes, we mean a toilet break. It is not easy to focus on a conversation when suddenly the only thing you can think about is how you need to answer the call of nature. The same can be true if you're too hot, if you're shivering with the cold, or if you're so hungry you think you may keel over. Any kind of physical discomfort can make it really hard to pay attention to what the other person is saying. It's better to be honest, take a quick break, and get back to them than to be barely listening to what might be an important conversation.

3. **Preoccupations.** Our ability to listen can be affected by things going on in our lives. This can create a situation where you're mentally multitasking. If your thoughts are even partly focused on your personal life, you're not going to be able to listen with the kind of attention we've been talking about. If you're not able to overcome those drifting thoughts, be honest with the person and let them know you're having trouble concentrating. Since we all experience those times, they should understand it doesn't mean you're not interested in what they're saying, just that this isn't the best time to discuss it.

4. **Closed minds.** This is a tough one to overcome. If your mind is firmly made up about something, you're not likely to give your full attention to a differing opinion, and even less likely

to genuinely consider its merits. In those cases, you may be missing a detail you *can* agree on or a bit of new information. Both of those can lead to an open discussion if you know how to listen and respond in a way that opens the door for communication.

The fact of the matter is that we all carry with us certain beliefs, influences, ideas, values, and biases. And those things can prevent us from developing the open-minded superpower component of communication.

Wait! Won't an Open Mind Make You Gullible and Easily Tricked?

Not at all. In fact, using critical thinking skills (coming in Chapter Four!), you'll find that the more you learn about other points of view, the better equipped you'll be to reach a well-informed opinion.

A potential bonus is this: if you're willing to open yourself up, to explore and rethink, you just might find that the other person will do the same. It may not change any viewpoints, but it shows respect when you're willing to listen and consider.

Open-Mindedness

The most important thing to remember is that you're in a conversation, not a verbal battle.

Here are some ways you can tell them apart:

Person in a Conversation	Person in a Verbal Battle
Is open to considering others' feelings, ideas, and opinions.	Quickly shuts down others' feelings, ideas, and opinions.
Encourages conversation by being willing to hear what others say.	Discourages conversation by stubbornly refusing to hear what others say.
Is attentive and respectful, whether they agree with the other viewpoint or not.	Is often rude and dismissive toward the other viewpoint.
Listens until the other person has finished speaking. Is mannerly in all aspects of the way they respond.	Interrupts by speaking or making faces or derisive sounds before the other person can finish speaking.

It's worth asking yourself two questions on this subject. (Don't worry, this isn't a surprise quiz — you know the answers.)

Which of these people do I enjoy talking with?

Which of these people do I want to be when talking to others?

A final word on this subject: even a good listener knows there are limits!

Chapter Three Activities

Individual Activities

Listen Up!

Sharpen your listening skills with this fun activity. Once you practice active listening, you'll see your ability to retain information get better and better!

Watch a ten-to-fifteen-minute segment of an informational show such as a nature documentary. (Be sure it's something you can pause and watch again.) At the end of the designated time, make notes in point form of the various things you learned. Then go back and rewatch. Did you record the facts given accurately? Were there any that you missed completely? On the second viewing, pay extra attention to the visual clues and details that could be helpful to you in remembering.

Listen Up Two!

This activity also involves the use of a show or movie. This time, you'll be working on your ability to identify feelings, so try to choose something with strong emotional elements. When you hit "play," turn your back so that you are only able to hear what is happening. Pay attention to voices — not only what is said but how — and to background sounds that may offer clues.

As you listen, make brief notes describing what you think each of the characters is feeling. When you've finished, replay the scene, but this time watch it. Does what you see support what you believe you heard?

When you understand the feelings involved, you're in a good position to consider ways you could show empathy. To do this, it may help to ask yourself, *Have I had experiences that allow me to feel some of what the character is feeling? What would I want someone to do for me if I was in that situation?*

Group Activities

Did You Hear?

Divide a group into two teams. Each team forms a line with two feet between each player. A moderator whispers a starter sentence to the first person in each line.

All sentences should begin with the phrase: "Did you hear that ..." as shown in the following samples.

Did you hear that ...

... flamingos can only eat when their heads are turned upside down?

... oak trees are struck by lightning more frequently than any other tree?

... when a bat flies out of a cave, it always starts its journey by turning left?

... a strawberry is the only fruit with all of the seeds growing on the outside?

The moderator starts the play by calling, "Go!"

The first person in line then steps to the second person in line and whispers the sentence. It must be quiet enough that no one else can hear. The next person does the same, and so on.

The last person writes what they heard on a slip of paper and passes it to the moderator.

The moderator reads each team's sentence aloud, followed by the original one.

Scoring is as follows:

✓ Two points are awarded to the team who gets the sentence to the last person in line the fastest.

✓ Perfect, word-for-word final sentence: Five points.

✓ Some words changed or missing but meaning still true: Three points.

✓ Original meaning didn't survive! Zero points.

Play may continue with new sentences for as long as the group likes, but the players should shuffle order for each round of play.

The team with the highest end score wins.

Catch That Word!

This game will help you to focus and to sharpen your listening skills.

Each person in the group will take a turn as the catcher. The catcher is sent away from the room while the others choose the secret word. (Common descriptive words are best.) The group also chooses a subject to talk about — it should be as general as possible. When the catcher returns, each person says one thing on the chosen subject, working the secret word into their sentence.

To keep it from being obvious, everyone should include several other descriptive words in what they say as well. For example, if the secret word is *small* and the subject is nature, a player might say,

"It's amazing to think that a tall, green plant started out as a small, brown seed."

The catcher stops play when they are ready to identify the secret word.

Scoring: Five points are added to the catcher's score for each time the secret word is said before they correctly identify it. In this game, the lowest score wins!

Chapter Three Rapid Recap

✓ Using body language such as eye contact or nodding can help indicate that you are actively listening.

✓ Avoid interrupting so you can process the whole message you are hearing.

✓ Recognize that your own opinions and biases may get in the way of feeling empathy for others.

✓ It is best not to judge someone on their reaction to something. Personal experiences, problems, or sensitivities can affect how they react.

✓ Physical issues such as tiredness or hunger can distract us from listening well.

✓ We can also be distracted when our minds are preoccupied with our own troubles.

-CHAPTER FOUR-

Reflect, Respond, Repeat

We bet you're amazed at what you've learned about communication so far. Maybe you're even thinking there can't possibly be anything else. After all, you're practically an expert on body language, conversation tips, and paying attention now. You know the ins and outs of talking and listening — what else is there?

Actually, quite a bit. There's processing what the other person said, considering what you want to say in response, and deciding *how* you want to say it. A good deal of that happens quickly, as you'd expect in a normal conversation.

Now and then, it actually happens just a little *too* quickly. We're talking about those times when your mouth races on ahead of your brain.

You know exactly what we mean by that, don't you! We've all been there — cringing at the memory of something we said. Unfortunately, there's no backspace or delete key in those instances. You can't undo words once they're out there.

What you *can* do is learn to be more mindful when you're speaking, especially in certain settings. Things that might be fine to say in a group of friends are not necessarily going to get the super-power stamp of approval in other circumstances.

Let's take a look at some common, yet avoidable, mistakes many of us make when we're in a situation where a little decorum is called for.

No Regrets!

We could avoid a lot of the cringeworthy moments in our lives if we took a few seconds to consider whether something we're about to say has the potential to turn around and kick us in the posterior. (Even if that word is new to you, we're betting you can figure out what it means.)

An excellent way to stop yourself from making remarks you may later regret is to keep your conversation respectful. Watch what you say and the way you say it. Be especially careful to avoid:

- Slang that your pals understand but that could puzzle and possibly offend others.
- Crude talk or insinuations – anything that has the potential to shock and embarrass. One thing it will *never* do is impress!
- Humor that could come across as offensive. Ditto with teasing.
- Sharp or angry responses. Keeping your cool gives you a distinct advantage over those who lose theirs!

Remember, showing respect will earn you respect in return. You will stand out as a young person with class, dignity, and intelligence. That's pretty much a guarantee!

Handling Conflict

We all get angry. But guess what? Anger is no friend of conversation. Speaking when you're riled up can unleash a tirade you'd never let out if you were calm and in full control of yourself. The result can be devastating. You may be left with bruised or broken relationships and other unhappy consequences, including more of those unpleasant memories that can haunt you years later.

Wouldn't it be great if you could avoid all that drama? We think you can. The secret in this case is knowing how to react *before* you find your temper starting to rise. It's a lot easier to think clearly and act wisely with a game plan solidly in place.

Here are a few things you can do when your annoyance is in danger of shifting into high gear:

1. **Know what ticks you off!** Learn to recognize the things that trigger your anger. We all have them. Not only does your temper flare, but there are often physical reactions as well. Tension, clenching of hands or teeth, rapid heartbeat — pay attention to what your body is telling you! Once you figure out what words and actions get under your skin, you'll be on your way to beating them. Remind yourself: *I control my emotions — no person or situation has the power to do that unless I let them.*

2. **Laugh it off.** Depending on the circumstances, you may want to try lightening the subject using humor or deflection.

3. **Breathe!** Take deep, abdominal breaths. Focusing on your breathing can be very calming.

4. **Open your mind.** Beware of overreacting or being close-minded toward what's being said.

5. **Think it through.** Examine thoughts and ideas logically instead of emotionally.

6. **Look for middle ground.** Try to find a point of agreement. It's possible a solution or compromise can help keep the peace.

7. **Disengage!** If all else fails, you may need to disengage. Suggest a time-out or a subject change. If you can't leave, and the other person won't stop, take away their ability to rile you up by refusing to respond. It's difficult for an argument to go on very long when there is only one side participating.

Conflict in Disguise: Passive-Aggressive Behavior

Sometimes anger wears a disguise, which is known as passive-aggressive behavior. This is when words and gestures that pretend to be harmless on the surface are actually expressing hostility in subtle or indirect ways.

It's likely you've seen this before, perhaps without realizing what it was. Think of it as anger's sneaky approach — the way it comes out when it's trying to pretend it's something else. Like humor, except the kind that has a mean undercurrent, such as, "Great haircut — I hear the homeless look is coming into style!"

Another example of passive-aggressive communication is muttering: those remarks a person makes under their breath — the ones you can't quite hear, but you still know they're critical or cutting. That's usually easy to confirm — just ask the person to repeat what they said. They'll likely laugh it off or say, "Never mind." But everyone still knows whatever they said wasn't kind, don't they?

And, of course, some muttered remarks are meant to be heard. "That's what you think" or "You should know" are examples most of us are familiar with. A fake cough that doesn't quite cover up "Lame," "As if," or something similar also falls into that category.

Sarcasm is also a type of passive-aggressive communication. With sarcasm, people pass off clearly hurtful remarks as jokes. Their words leave a sting, but if challenged they may claim they were "just kidding." They might even act offended at the idea they meant to be unkind.

Passive-aggressive "compliments" work the same way. Imagine how you'd feel if someone said something like, "Love your new shoes! It's great how you don't care that something isn't fashionable anymore!" That's not really a compliment, is it?

When you understand how it works, you'll know a passive-aggressive comment is usually covering up anger or jealousy. That should help you be aware of what may sometimes tempt you to speak in a passive-aggressive way yourself.

It's also true that anyone can have a bad day and say something out of character for that reason. Do your best to remember that, and don't judge them too harshly, even if they've been unkind to you.

How Should You Respond to Passive-Aggressive Statements?

- If it's something minor, you might just ignore it. A reaction could just encourage more passive-aggressive words and behaviors. If you can, move on to a new subject or use humor to deflect the tension.
- Try to keep your cool. Those verbal jabs are meant to hurt and anger, so when you don't let them get to you, you've kept them from succeeding. Take a few breaths, but don't take the bait!
- If it's too hurtful or embarrassing to ignore or sidestep, go ahead and address what was said directly. But do your best to speak in a calm and respectful way, because that's the most likely way to prevent escalation. Focus on the intent to hurt, not the content of whatever was said. Try a simple response such as, "I hope you didn't mean to be unkind, but what you just said was hurtful."

Speaking of things that can hurt others in a conversation, let's talk about gossip ...

What's Good about Gossip?

Answering that question won't take long. There's *nothing* good about gossip. It's a distasteful type of communication that you should sidestep whenever possible.

Wait! Isn't gossip just harmless information sharing? Let's take a closer look. Gossip has a well-earned reputation for being mean. It's what people say behind someone else's back, and it's usually negative and spiteful. Even worse, gossip is often filled with exaggerations, half-truths, and outright lies.

So what makes people do it? There are a few things that motivate someone to spread rumors. There's the attention it gets them and the thrill of being the first one to share a story. Some people get a strange kind of enjoyment from talking about the misfortunes and failings of others, and some are just busybodies, plain and simple.

So, are all gossips bad people? Not at all. Gossiping may be an attempt for a person to fit in. It could also be a habit they've developed because others around them do it. Even so, it's not a good or kind thing to do. And anyone can break a bad habit if they try.

Even something that is true can be gossip. Sharing things that are private (sometimes even about yourself!) can be terribly tempting. The problem is, if *you* couldn't keep a secret, why would you expect anyone else to? Very few people will respect your request to tell no one — and in no time, that private matter will be known far and wide. Don't be the one responsible for disclosing information that's personal or sensitive.

Even at its least harmful, gossip falls into the not-your-story-to-tell and none-of-your-business categories. If you're spreading stories about someone without their knowledge and consent, you're gossiping. It's a habit that will damage your reputation and keep others from trusting you.

You see, there's one thing everybody knows about a gossip, and it's this: if they're talking *to* you about someone else behind their back, they're also talking *about* you to others when you're not around. Gossips are often seen as people who can't be trusted. And even when their intention isn't harmful, their careless words can hurt.

There's a lot of it out there — we know that. But it can be beaten. Stopping this practice starts with you. It starts with you not spreading it and not encouraging it from others. Shut it down when you can.

How? Show them that what they're doing is not okay. Use your body language to lean back and look away to let them know you're not a fan. Don't be afraid to contradict hurtful comments and defend the gossip's target when you can.

Letting a gossip know you're not comfortable talking about someone who's not there to speak for themselves or simply saying you'd rather talk about something else are simple but highly effective ways of taking away the power of this harmful habit. It might even be that appealing to their better nature will help encourage them to stop gossiping.

What Do YOU Talk About?

"Great minds discuss ideas, average minds discuss events, small minds discuss people."

– Anonymous

Leaving Doors Open

Is it really necessary to learn all of these things and develop these communication skills? Is it seriously such a big deal if you're just a tiny bit obnoxious now and then?

Maybe not. But on the other hand, maybe it is. You see, you never know where life might lead you. Someone you acted boorishly in front of today could reappear in your life in the most unexpected way down the road. Do you really want to risk having the bad impression you made today cling to you like a lovesick orangutan through a whole lot of tomorrows?

It's a bit like closing a door, locking it, and tossing the key into the gutter, only to someday discover you'd like to go back inside. Be wise enough not to cause problems in your own future because of unsavory communication today.

Moving Forward ... Taking Time to Reflect

We live in an instant kind of world. Immediate access, speedy delivery, quick, quick, quick. We don't like to wait, and for many of us, that means we've put aside a highly valuable practice — namely, pondering.

Think about it! We're often in such a rush that we accept ideas and opinions without checking whether they're true or if they even make sense. And once we decide what to believe, it's easy to close ourselves off to information that might challenge it.

How wise is that? On a scale of one to ten, it rates a great big zero. It's human nature, though. We don't like to be mistaken, and admitting gullibility isn't easy. But you know what? Most people respect and admire a person with the courage to stand up and say, "I was wrong. I looked at the facts, and I've changed my mind."

Which leads us to ...

Critical Thinking

Pssst. Have you heard about the giant mutant mosquitoes that drained all the blood from an entire herd of wildebeests?

You haven't? Well, it was gruesome! We even saw pictures online proving it. Professor Shamquack, who discovered the mutation, says these flying monsters could easily wipe out life on this planet in less than a year. Our only chance for survival is to wear an invisible shield when we go outside. Luckily, the article has a link to buy the shield!

Did you believe us? Of course, you didn't. But *why* didn't you?

You didn't believe it because you used something called critical thinking. This is the term for examining information in a way that allows you to reach a reasonable conclusion. You considered the details (which probably didn't take more than a couple of seconds) and dismissed it as the nonsense it was.

But what if you saw the pictures we'd mentioned? What if the pictures were convincingly realistic? What if you found other stories reporting the same thing — and they all looked totally legit? What if you saw a video of Professor Shamquack explaining, in scientific-sounding detail, how the mosquitoes mutated and showing complicated charts about the danger they pose to life on planet Earth? What if some of your family members and close friends were convinced it was true? Suppose they talked about it day after day after day? And what if they mocked you for believing anyone who insisted the whole thing was a hoax?

What then? Could you be persuaded?

Critical thinking is essential when you're faced with conflicting information and opinions. You already know that not everything you hear is true. But a lot of false information contains *some* truth, and that can be confusing. Knowing how to apply critical thinking will help you sort out facts from folly.

What Exactly Is Critical Thinking?

In short, critical thinking means analyzing. It's a system of examining information in order to figure out what's logical.

What does it matter? Why can't everyone just believe whatever seems right to them?

Suppose you're responsible for mixing the ingredients in a medication, and the formula calls for two parts of one ingredient and one part of another. Let's say you firmly believe that numbers are irrelevant, so you dump in random amounts instead. That could bring about harmful, even tragic, results.

Take a Deep Breath --
It's not easy to think critically when you're angry, upset, or even joyous and excited. Make sure you examine subjects when your emotions aren't leading the way!

QUICK TIP

So yes, it matters. And for many reasons. Here are some of the ways in which the ability to use critical thinking can be important, even vital, to you:

✓ **Making better decisions.** The stronger your critical thinking skills are, the less you'll be persuaded by others' opinions. You'll gain confidence and will no longer feel the need to second-guess yourself. You'll be able to consider the pros and cons and make rational life choices for important matters such as careers and major purchases. And you'll be much less likely to fall for scams or cons when they come along.

✓ **Having opinions others value.** We all tend to turn to people we know to be rational when we're looking for an opinion or a bit of advice. As a critical thinker, you'll be able to offer exactly that kind of level-headed, well-thought-out point of view when it's needed.

✓ **Impact on relationships.** Because relationships are ruled, at least in part, by emotions, it might surprise you to know how essential critical thinking is, even in this aspect of your life. The ability to see both sides of an issue is helpful for resolving conflicts. You will also learn to recognize when someone is being insincere or manipulative.

✓ **Self-confidence.** Being able to evaluate your abilities helps you improve your talents. It also serves to identify weaknesses and what you can do about them in order to gain poise and self-assurance.

Take the time to learn the key components of critical thinking:

1. **Pick up on errors, gaps, and inconsistent patterns in reasoning.** This means watching for faulty statements. A simple example would be: "This is true because everyone knows it's been proven." That statement is like a circle where the first and last parts, "This is true" and "it's been proven," seem to prop each other up, but neither is supported by any actual facts.

2. **Consider the idea you're exploring in a structured and organized manner.** Is it built on a solid foundation? What if someone offered to sell you a ticket to a boat ride on a floating

lake? Before you get out your cash, you might want to ask yourself how a lake could float!

3. **Understand what creates a connection between ideas.** It's very common for faulty arguments to claim one thing backs up another when in fact there is little or nothing to support such a link. Imagine someone told you, "All smart people like apple pie." They might even show you some "evidence" to prove it, but that wouldn't make it true.

4. **Determine the importance and relevance of arguments and ideas.** Be wary of supporting evidence that's weak or has little to do with the subject. These are "grasping at straws" statements that are offered as proof but that prove nothing. "Don't eat peaches! My cousin ate a peach, and she had a headache for the rest of the day!" Sorry about your cousin's headache, but there's nothing to back up the idea that the peach caused it. Watch out when someone claims cause and effect without *proving* the connection.

5. **Adopt a systematic method for examining information.** The best way to determine truth is to research any questions you have until you're fully satisfied with the answers. This will happen when you can say with confidence the research you did looked at all sides of a question, sought information from reliable sources, and produced answers that make sense.

6. **Consider how biases (theirs and yours) affect beliefs and conclusions.** If you lean toward accepting or rejecting an idea, you're likely to favor evidence that supports what you want to be true. Do your best to examine information from a neutral point of view so that your own and others' biases will not sway your reasoning.

7. **Think ahead!** Some ideas sound great until you see the potential problems that could come out of them later. Take the time to consider what ripple effects there might be.

The ability to be objective, to analyze and evaluate subjects and situations, will be of value to you in more ways than you can imagine! Once you understand and adopt critical thinking, you'll be harder to fool and won't be easily taken in by fraud or manipulation.

Even so, there may be times when you're just not sure. You've seen photos, videos, and articles that really look legitimate. It can all be incredibly confusing, but there *is* something that can help you sort it all out, and that is *looking at the source!*

Where'd You Hear THAT?

If you spend any time on social media, you'll know there are a lot of conflicting opinions out there on, well, practically everything! You've probably seen some pretty wild ideas, and you may have found yourself scratching your head, trying to decide what's real and what isn't. There are many false stories floating around, and the people who create them have developed sophisticated ways to make them look and sound convincing.

Naturally, you're going to use your newly honed critical thinking skills, but you'll also want to take a careful look at the source in those cases. Whether the source is an individual or a group, here are some tips to help you decide if it's credible:

✓ Other sources back up or verify the information presented. If it's nowhere on mainstream media, consider that a huge red flag. And don't let yourself be persuaded that millions of mainstream news sources have all conspired to keep this information from you. Seriously, why would they? (There's never a sensible answer to that, incidentally, although we've heard some pretty far-fetched theories.) Check out claims and statistics — there are many good websites that provide solid fact-checking results and can speed this process for you.

✓ Don't let yourself be fooled by websites that are designed to look like legitimate news sources. Dig deeper into their history. Check out the author of the article and their background. Examine the quality of any photos. Pay attention to whether the site looks cluttered. Look at the date of publication — if there isn't one, that's a hint it may be false. Beware of clickbait — another telltale sign that it's not genuine news reporting!

✓ Trustworthy news sources are objective. They offer full information from all sides in an unbiased manner. They are reporting facts, not trying to persuade, mock, or incite fear. Any of those tactics are significant red flags!

If the information you're wondering about doesn't pass inspection in these areas, you can be reasonably sure it's at least partially false. It may fool other people, but it's not going to fool you!

When you've reached a conclusion, you may find it tempting to challenge others who have fallen for false information. This is rarely a good idea unless that person is truly open to examining the facts. More often, it will lead to a disagreement that will remain unresolved and could create hard feelings. Often, in such situations, it's best to agree to disagree and move on to some other subject.

As you can see, developing strong communication skills requires more than words and gestures. Some of the most important components are going on behind the scenes, analyzing, deducing, and reacting. That process helps you avoid wrong assumptions, verbal blunders, and other mistakes that can be difficult to fix.

Rise to the challenge!

Chapter Four Activities

Individual Activities

Visualization

Visualization is a powerful tool that can make a difference in your ability to handle conflict. To practice it, choose a quiet setting where it's unlikely you'll be disturbed. Begin with a moment or two of abdominal breathing.

Close your eyes and imagine yourself in a situation of potential conflict. See yourself remaining calm and in control of your emotions. "Hear" your voice responding in a firm but respectful manner. (You may find it helpful to review phrases that others have found effective in such situations.)

Visualization can help you build the confidence and skills needed to remain composed during times of conflict.

Expert or Imposter?

These days, anyone can create a professional-looking website and claim to be an expert on a topic. Their arguments may sound convincing, but do they really have the credentials to make the claims they are making? Or are they presenting their own opinions (or what they *want* to be true) as factual?

Use a search engine to find someone speaking on a subject you are interested in. Now use your sleuthing skills to figure out how accurate the information may be, who the author is, what organizations they are affiliated with, and what biases they may have.

You can use these steps to get started:

1. Check the date of the presentation. Is it recent? If it is a few years old, the information will be out-of-date.

2. Google the speaker's name. (If there are too many people with the same name, add the presentation topic to the search.) Is the speaker connected with a college or university? Do they have a degree related to the topic of the presentation? What other talks, articles, books, or publications have they authored?

3. If there is a transcript of the talk available, or an article related to the talk, check to see if there are sources for information listed at the end. This will show you how diligent the author was in finding accurate, proven facts and not just spouting their own opinions as fact.

4. Is the author associated with an organization either mentioned in the talk or found in your Google search? Check to see if that organization is objective and scientific in its mission.

5. Examine the website that is hosting the author's presentation. Does the information on it seem to be slanted or biased in one direction or does it show many different perspectives when presenting material?

With this information, what is your view on the credibility of the speaker? How seriously will you take what they said?

Group Activities

Fact or Opinion?

Sometimes opinions are presented as if they are proven facts. An opinion is simply how someone feels about a subject. A fact is a detail that can be proven with scientific evidence. It is important to be able to distinguish between the two so you can determine how much weight to give the information being included in a conversation, speech, or debate.

In this activity, a group is given a series of statements that are either fact or opinion. The statements can either be handed out on individual pages for participants to mark with an *F* or an *O* or they can be written on a board and a show of hands can identify them as fact or opinion.

A discussion can help participants discover ways to better figure out one from the other and learn why we can be easily swayed when listening to a very persuasive speaker.

Some sample fact or opinion statements could be:

1. All planets are spheres.
2. It's better to live in France than Germany.
3. Dodo birds are extinct.
4. Facebook is better than Twitter because there is no character limit on posts.
5. Dancing is more fun than skateboarding.
6. The highest mountain on Earth is Mount Everest.
7. Seatbelt laws don't work.

8. Gold is heavier than silver.

9. The most beautiful flower is the rose.

10. Viruses are bigger than air molecules.

Think About It!

Prepare questions for discussion on slips of paper, which can be folded and placed in a container. The group then begins by drawing out one paper and reading the question. Each group member who wishes to offer a point of view may do so for a maximum of three minutes. In between speakers, allow a short pause (thirty to sixty seconds) for everyone to consider what has just been said.

When those who wish to speak have done so, open the floor for respectful discussion. Group members may share which statements they found most persuasive and which ones raised questions.

Questions should be general in nature, not based on current or controversial events. The intention is to speculate, not establish a "correct" answer. Here are some samples:

✓ What makes someone a "good person"?

✓ What is truth? Can opposing beliefs both be true?

✓ Is artificial intelligence actually intelligent?

✓ Is it possible for freedom to be absolute?

✓ Will time travel ever actually happen?

Chapter Four Rapid Recap

✓ Take a moment to check what you are about to say before blurting out something you may regret later!

✓ Recognize the things that trigger your anger and use breathing techniques, humor, a short pause, or seeing another perspective to help avoid an angry reaction.

✓ Learn to identify passive-aggressive speech and plan a calm response.

✓ Don't use passive-aggressive language yourself.

✓ Gossip can destroy your reputation and people's trust in you.

✓ Use critical thinking skills to examine information before you form an opinion.

Up Close and Virtual

Virtual connections have become a regular part of most of our lives. It's the next best thing to being in the same room with family, friends, and coworkers. In a sense, the rules for virtual communication are very much like the ones that serve us when we're actually face-to-face. There are differences too, of course, some of which are beneficial and some of which need a little extra care. And we aren't just talking about accidentally standing up when your off-camera bod is clad only in skivvies.

The Perils of Posting: Social Media and More

We discussed earlier how easy it can be to blurt out the wrong thing during conversations. The same is true when you're communicating digitally. Lots of people connect with friends, relatives, and

/89

even employers by email, by texting, through social media platforms, or on any number of apps. And why not? There is a huge
advantage to being able to connect with people around the globe
in an instant. Besides, we can't deny that hearing the *ping* that a
message has arrived gets the adrenaline pumping.

The ease and speed with which we can connect with others
digitally can offer additional advantages as well. Help can be sum-
moned immediately in an emergency. (Imagine how many lives
have been saved because of this!) A quick text to a parent when
your ride doesn't show up or a DM (direct message) to a friend to
change your meetup time at the last minute, check the due date of a
project, or get a suddenly needed contact number — these are just
a few of the ways instant messaging is handy.

QUICK TIP

Is It Too Late? --
You cannot always go back and edit a message or post. It is a good idea to get into the habit of rereading everything you wrote before you hit "send."

There are other benefits to connecting digitally. One is something you can't avoid when meeting in person, and that is people judging you on your looks before getting to know you. It's not a good feeling, right? There is so much more to you than your face or clothes. Wouldn't it be great for people to listen to your thoughts and ideas first to decide whether they like you, want to spend more time with you, or even want to hire you? Well, with digital conversations, they can. So many apps allow you to use an avatar and a username. These let you choose how to present yourself to the world and give people a chance to know who you are.

You may have heard of your parents or grandparents having pen pals (people in another city or even country whom they wrote letters to but often never met). Some of these friendships lasted a lifetime. Today's digital world offers the same idea, but on a bigger scale. Social media sites and apps often have groups and group chats. Pick any subject, hobby, or topic you can think of, and there's bound to be a group of like-minded people who get together online to chat and share news and ideas.

Ever get frustrated that your meetup with friends, study group, visit with grandparents, or other plans got cancelled for reasons outside of your control? Well, with video calls, things that might affect an in-person get-together won't keep you from connecting with your friends and family. Just grab a drink and snack and settle in for a long talk at your computer.

Of course, nothing is perfect, and digital communication has its flaws. Those long, cozy online chats are great until your connection gets interrupted. Modern technology sometimes fails — cell towers go down, Wi-Fi gets disrupted, weather affects satellites, or, horror of horrors, you might have limited bandwidth. There goes that heart-to-heart — or, worse, a frozen screen just as a big announcement was about to be shared with you! But have no fear, these problems are well known and happen to everyone, so people are usually understanding about them.

What they might not understand is if your message is full of typos, misspellings, bad grammar, and abbreviations that are unfamiliar to them. And you want the person you're messaging to understand what you have to say, right?

TTYL (Talk to You Later!)

Abbreviations have gained tremendous popularity in digital communication. They offer speed and convenience and can be especially useful in platforms where the number of words or characters are limited!

In spite of the advantages, it's wise to use abbreviations with care. Why? Because not everyone is familiar with the various meanings. BRB (be right back), FWIW (for what it's worth), or IMHO (in my humble opinion) are only valuable shortcuts when the other person understands them. Be mindful that when you include abbreviations, there's a risk your meaning may be missed or misunderstood.

Communicating in the digital world has other drawbacks. Perhaps the biggest one is that words spoken in person don't have anything close to the reach or staying power of words that have been sent off into the electronic world. Those things aren't easy to get rid of! In fact, they can echo on and on into the future in incredibly far-reaching ways. Once you send a message electronically, there's no guarantee it won't reappear through a share, repost, screenshot, or some other method.

And what of private messages sent by text, email, and other apps and programs? You can delete them from *your* system, but you can't remove them from the side that received them. So, let's figure out how we can all be a little wiser about expressing ourselves digitally.

Oh, yes, we know the urge can be powerful indeed! A funny remark, an angry challenge — there are so many times it's tempting to show the world how witty you are, or perhaps informed, indignant, caring, indifferent ... really, the list of reasons for treating the world to your opinions is practically endless.

Luckily, most of those comments are never going to give you a moment of grief. But most is not all.

Think about it! What might seem funny or justified to you today could lead to problems down the road. You don't need that.

Here's a list of things to consider when you're about to text, post, or send any message that might not pass the "safe to say" test:

✓ Is there any discrimination in what I'm about to say?

✓ Am I (intentionally or accidentally) insulting or mocking anyone? Would I feel okay about someone saying the same thing about me?

✓ Is this information verified? Or might I be spreading something that is false?

✓ Are there unpleasant ways this could be interpreted?

✓ Am I spreading gossip or sharing someone's personal affairs?

By the way, some people get awfully "brave" when they're hiding behind an electronic device. They say things they'd never say to someone's face. This is cowardly and detestable. If you're ever even a little bit tempted to write something you probably wouldn't say in person — don't! You're better than that!

Spell-Check and Autocorrect: Should You Trust Them?

Spell-check can make you lazy, or it can make you smarter! Yes, it's true. It depends how you use it.

If you just accept whatever spell-check suggests, your compositions are bound to contain things you didn't mean to say. Don't assume spell-check is always right — it absolutely isn't. It's a tool that makes suggestions to help you, but you should still be doing the thinking and making the right choices. If you're paying attention and making sure you accept only words that reflect what you intended to write, your brain will be analyzing and getting sharper. It will also be absorbing the correct spellings for future use.

Are tortillas glutton free?

Depends on how many you eat, I guess.

I meant gluten!

Autocorrect, on the other hand, is a bit cheeky. While spell-check makes suggestions for you to choose from, autocorrect just goes ahead and puts in what it thinks you meant to say. Which is how we end up sending messages that say peculiar things like:

✓ It's Toby's turn to put out the cabbage.

✓ She's just sweating on the couch.

✓ I can't find my labyrinth.

✓ The leaves are wrestling in the breeze.

✓ I'm meeting Mom at the stakeout.

Autocorrect can be helpful, but you've got to keep a sharp eye on it. If you don't, it's bound to engage in some word shenanigans at your expense.

Best Practices for Video Calls

You might think that because you can see each other, video calls are practically the same as in-person conversations. While some things are similar, video calls have their own problems and benefits. Let's start with the obvious — you can see each other. Is that a problem or a benefit? Well, that depends. Seeing the other person allows you to use some of those body language interpreting skills you picked up earlier in this book. Even if you can just see from the shoulders up, there's a lot of information in the eyes, eyebrows, mouth, neck, and shoulders. Are they shrugging? Yawning? Raising their eyebrows? Frowning? Rolling their eyes? You can learn a lot about how your messages are being received by watching your screen.

On the other hand, you won't see much body language if you spend your time staring at your own image to see how you look to others. Don't think we don't know everyone does this!

Don't forget the importance of the nonverbal signals you're sending too. Do your best to make virtual connections as meaningful as possible. Looking at your camera is as close as you can get to making eye contact with the other person. A little hand talk (thumbs-up, silent clapping, jazz hands, etc.) will add depth and clarification to your words. And of course, facial expressions will help round out the experience. All of these things affect the impression others will have of you online.

Of course, you *do* need to take a quick look at yourself now and then to make sure you haven't had a wardrobe malfunction, been turned into a blur by a fickle camera, or run into any other visual issue. But other than that, try to keep yourself focused on the camera or screen. If your gaze is wandering out the window, off to one side or the other, or worse, down at your phone — well, you know the message that's sending. It tells the other person you're not interested enough in the conversation to give them your attention. And that's not the impression you want to give, because it's rude, and you're not a rude person.

Even in virtual settings where there are several people joining a conversation, others are going to notice if your actions are inattentive. Instead of behaving impolitely to *one* person, you're parading bad manners for the whole group to see.

QUICK TIP

Keep It Private ---
Always turn your video off if you have personal issues to take care of. You might think those motions aren't in camera range, but they often are. Remember, no one wants to see you blowing your nose, scratching an itch, or getting something out of your teeth.

The same rule goes for the microphone. Hit the mute button if there's something noisy going on. No one will appreciate it if what they're saying is interrupted by you scolding your dog for eating your slippers, a truck going by an open window, or someone forgetting this isn't an ideal time to turn on the vacuum. The list of possible background sounds is practically endless, but remember it includes personal eruptions such as sneezing, coughing, and other body sounds that no one needs to hear — you know what we mean!

And while we're on the topic of what the camera sees, check your background! Right or wrong, people will form opinions about you based on what they see. Is it messy? Is there anything embarrassing? Might the person on the other side of the conversation see (or even *think* they see) something illegal or offensive? Before you connect with a friend, your grandmother, or, heaven forbid, a prospective boss, take a critical look around. When possible, try to prevent distractions. Close the door so your pet emu doesn't wander in by accident. Set your phone to mute. Let people in the house know you'll be busy with a call.

Remember, people can record video calls. You don't need something embarrassing being captured in a clip or screenshot. Those things have a way of reappearing at the worst possible times!

Best Practices for Written Digital Communication

Emailing, texting, posting, tweeting, captioning — there are lots of ways to communicate with words online. But these conversations are not without potential pitfalls! Taking a few simple precautions can prevent some serious sender's remorse.

First of all, resist the urge to send a message before reading it over. And when you read it, try to do so from the recipient's point of view. It's your one chance to catch the mistakes that could cause your message to be misinterpreted. Ask yourself how it may come across to someone in a bad mood or a person who's sensitive about a certain topic. Realize that what you say may live forever.

Avoid "vague posting," which is a term used to describe texts, captions, or posts that hint at something exciting or horrible or embarrassing without giving any information. The idea is to create curiosity, but most people just find it annoying. It's not uncommon for others to stop responding to messages from those who make a habit of vague posting. So don't be that person. Just imagine, after driving everyone away with that disappointing clickbait, you suddenly have a real emergency. Your frantic "Call me!" or "I need to talk to you!" might get an eye roll instead of a speedy response.

Earlier, we talked about changing the tone of your words when speaking to someone. A strong tone can help express excitement or anger. A soft tone is calm and convincing. But how do you get tone into digital conversations? One way is the USE OF ALL CAPS. Sorry, we mean the use of all caps. Did you find it hard to read in all caps? Most people do. That's because it seems like shouting. If you use it for an entire message, people begin to feel attacked. So, check that you haven't accidentally left the caps lock on and keep your written tone polite and respectful.

All the Feels

The little digital images called emojis can help convey the feelings that words without body language cannot. They can change the whole tone or meaning of a text or post. But we're sure you know their use has a time and place. Friends, family, and classmates will find them cute and funny — but if there's no personal relationship with the person you're messaging (such as a teacher or a friend's parent), emojis could backfire in unexpected ways.

Chapter Five Activities

Individual Activities

Correct Punctuation Can Save Lives, Stop Crime, and More!

With the limited characters of some texting platforms and apps, punctuation was one of the first things to get left behind. But punctuation is often vital to understanding. Punctuation marks aren't just squiggles on the page; they each have a function. Punctuation includes:

- ✓ Period (.) — We're pretty sure you know this means the end of a sentence!
- ✓ Comma (,) — It instructs you to pause and maybe take a breath. It also separates items in a list.
- ✓ Colon (:) — It is often used at the beginning of a list, just like at the beginning of this list!
- ✓ Semicolon (;) — It can join two connected sentences such as, "We left at sunrise; the weather looked promising."
- ✓ Exclamation mark (!) — It shows strong feelings. Sometimes it is overused!!!!! (See what we did there?)
- ✓ Question mark (?) — Pretty well known. It indicates a question. Or confusion.

So now that you've had a little refresher, can you add punctuation to these sentences so they mean what they were intended to say?

LET'S EAT GRANDPA

STOP DUCKS CROSSING

HELP A CROOK

TODAY WE WILL PRACTICE BOWLING STUDENTS

GOATS PLEASE CLOSE GATE

I'M SORRY YOU'RE RIGHT

GRANDMA LOVES COOKING HER GOLDFISH AND HER FAMILY

QUIET CHILDREN SLEEPING

NO JAYWALKING OFFENDERS WILL BE FINED

Punctuation Solutions for Correct Punctuation Can Save Lives, Stop Crime, and More!

LET'S EAT, GRANDPA!

STOP! DUCKS CROSSING.

HELP! A CROOK!

TODAY WE WILL PRACTICE BOWLING, STUDENTS.

GOATS! PLEASE CLOSE GATE.

I'M SORRY. YOU'RE RIGHT.

GRANDMA LOVES COOKING, HER GOLDFISH, AND HER FAMILY.

QUIET! CHILDREN SLEEPING.

NO JAYWALKING. OFFENDERS WILL BE FINED.

#Hashtags

Hashtags are a label attached to a post to link it to similar ideas, emotions, or groups. No one likes a post that has a hashtag after every word. But using hashtags can enhance the message you are trying to convey.

For example, see how the message "Family dinner tomorrow" changes with hashtags:

✓ "Family dinner tomorrow #excited"

✓ "Family dinner tomorrow #saveme"

✓ "Family dinner tomorrow #stretchypants"

Try adding two different hashtags to these messages to change their meaning:

"Museum field trip day #_____"

"Museum field trip day #_____"

"Last day of school #_____"

"Last day of school #_____"

"Tacos for supper #_____"

"Tacos for supper #_____"

"My dog ate my homework #_____"

"My dog ate my homework #_____"

"World Cup starts tomorrow #_____"

"World Cup starts tomorrow #_____"

Group Activities

To Text or Not to Text?

These days, we're doing more texting than ever before. It is the most popular form of communication — two billion people are using it worldwide. But sometimes, texting has replaced a face-to-face exchange where maybe it shouldn't have.

It's a good idea to consider which situations should be handled by text and which shouldn't. Have your group consider the situations listed below. Discuss whether texting is Always, Sometimes, or Never an appropriate way to deal with each scenario. If opinions vary, a vote may be the best way to establish the general consensus on what's best.

1. Cancel an appointment with your dentist.

2. Invite a friend to a party.

3. Complain about your teacher.

4. Send directions to your house.

5. Wish someone a happy birthday.

6. Let a neighbor know their dog pooped in your yard.

7. Send a password.

8. Schedule a nail or hair appointment.

9. Cancel plans with a friend at the last minute.

10. Ask if you can borrow something — try different scenarios with this one! What you want to borrow, and from whom, will almost certainly affect your answer.

Emoji Strings

Emojis are another way to enhance your posts. But you can muddle your message if they aren't used carefully. Emojis can either clarify or confuse. This activity can help remind us of just how powerful these tiny images can be.

Divide participants into two groups. One group at a time, have one member create a message using only a string of emojis on a computer or a phone, by drawing on a board, or using cutout images. Time how long it takes their team members to correctly decode the emojis. After all participants on both teams have had a turn, the team with the shortest decoding time wins!

Chapter Five Rapid Recap

✓ Remember that what you post, text, or send electronically may live forever, so be aware of what you create.

✓ Avoid insulting people, mocking, or spreading gossip online.

✓ Don't assume spell-check or autocorrect will fix your mistakes correctly — always reread your messages before you hit "send" or "post."

✓ Be mindful of what others will hear or see around you when you make video calls.

✓ Follow the accepted rules about written digital messages, such as avoiding ALL CAPS and using emojis in proper settings.

-CHAPTER SIX-

Finishing Touches

Have you ever watched a master craftsperson at work? It can be fascinating to see how they take raw material — a chunk of wood, for example — and work and shape it until it's a work of art. If you pay careful attention, you'll notice that what they're forming and shaping looks pretty good as they near the end of their work. But then something magic happens. They complete the finishing touches, smoothing and polishing, and suddenly, just like magic, their handiwork goes from good to *great*.

Finishing touches make the difference in a lot of things, and communication happens to be one of them. For all you've learned, it's the extra effort you put in at the end that's going to turn you into a genuinely great communicator.

Let's take a look at a few of those finishing touches.

Putting a Lid on Potty Mouth

First of all, what do we mean by "potty mouth"? Actually, there are lots of things that fit into that category. Profanity, obscenity, vulgarity, derogatory and racist remarks ... the list goes on. Racist and other discriminatory remarks are never okay, even among friends. Whether they're made in a hurtful way or intended to be humorous, such comments can shape attitudes and reinforce negative thinking. You're smart enough to know what words, expressions, and phrases are considered offensive — and *that* is really the key word. Because what we're talking about in general is language that offends.

If you're genuinely not sure if something fits this list, ask yourself: *Would a grandparent, a teacher, or a friend's parent consider it respectful or disrespectful if I said this to them?*

There are a lot of reasons people use this kind of language. And it's not our job to judge what is and isn't okay for you to say in casual settings with people you know well and are comfortable with. Instead, we'd like to help you figure out the ways it affects your communication, because, after all, that's what this book is all about.

There are a lot of reasons people use unsavory words. Here are some of them — please consider which boxes you'd tick when you're in an everyday social setting with chums.

It's okay to use potty mouth if ...	Never	Sometimes	Always
Everyone around me talks that way.			
It makes people laugh.			
I do it out of habit.			
I'm angry.			
I hurt myself.			
It sounds cool.			
These are my go-to words to describe everything.			
I want to insult someone.			
I'm having an argument.			

Now go back to the chart and decide how you'd answer if you were in a less casual situation, such as meeting a sports hero, getting assistance from a salesperson, or talking to an adult you just met.

And what about on social media, in emails, in text messages, or in written reports?

Chances are, your answers will vary depending on the circumstances. Hanging out with your friends is one thing, while other situations can be quite another. The main thing to remember is that your words communicate more than just meaning — they also create an impression of who you are. It's important to be aware of that in the way you speak.

The Perils of Potty Mouth

Maybe you already know there are dangers and drawbacks involved in the use of questionable language. But do you know all of them, and have you considered how they reflect on you from different points of view? For example:

✓ Slipups! If something becomes too habitual, it's likely to sneak out sometimes when you really, really wish it hadn't. Imagine letting loose a string of cuss words with an elderly grandparent nearby.

✓ Draw the line. There are some words that are *never* okay because their nature is so offensive or vulgar. Consider them beneath you — you're classier than that.

✓ Even informal workplaces have standards of acceptable language — keep that in mind on the job!

✓ Your vocabulary can become stunted if you use the same words all the time, and that includes this kind of talk. Don't limit your brain, especially since the constant use of bad language doesn't exactly make you sound smart. It just doesn't! Pay attention the next time you're with someone who uses the same crude words over and over. Is their conversation inspiring, interesting, and intelligent? Chances are it's none of those things. That's because the opportunity to inject depth and meaning into what you say is lost without the right words to carry them.

Taking the Stage: Public Speaking

The correct term for the fear of speaking in public is glossophobia, and if you suffer from it, you're not alone. In fact, three out of four people (or 75 percent) are affected by this particular phobia to one extent or another. Some are mildly nervous, while others experience a full-blown feeling of panic. But whether speaking in front of a group of people gives you slight anxiety or you find yourself dry mouthed, sweating, and gulping air while your heart pounds, know that it's a fear that can be overcome.

If you're able to tame those jitters enough to speak in public, your symptoms are most likely something you can conquer on your own. In that case, you'll find that the more often you do it, the easier it will get, until it's hardly an issue at all. You can find tips online for various ways to make the whole process easier using visualization, breathing exercises, and more.

However, even if your fear is debilitating and causes you distress you can't overcome on your own, there's still hope. There are professionals who can help. And if seeking treatment is a path you choose, the good news is that experts tell us the success rate is most encouraging.

Ready, Set, Speak!

Once you're ready for your debut on the stage, there are things you can do to increase your confidence. Let's say, for example, that you've been asked to give a presentation about anteaters.

First of all, knowing your subject is key. Learn everything you can about anteaters and then prepare your talk to include basic information as well as details that will hold listeners' attention. Your audience is likely to be surprised to hear that giant anteaters have no teeth, or that they gobble down as many as thirty thousand ants in a day. Knowing you're going to share things that are genuinely interesting is one of the greatest confidence boosters there is.

Be sure to wear something appropriate. Imagine stepping out on stage only to realize you didn't need to rent that tux to talk to your school's hiking club. That said, be sure whatever you *are* wearing is neat and clean. Stand with your shoulders back, your chin up, and your eyes looking out over the room. Good posture gives you an assured look.

If you're speaking for a certain length of time, you'll want to practice to be sure your presentation doesn't drag on too long or leave a gap of twenty loooooong, empty minutes to fill at the end. Besides helping smooth out the rough spots, practicing will help you remember what you plan to say. Visualizing is also helpful because it creates an expectation of success, and your brain responds well to positive reinforcement.

No matter how prepared you are, take an outline with key points and prompts. Just having that in front of you can help ease concerns about forgetting something. If you do need to refer to your outline, you can do so naturally by pausing for effect or taking a sip of water. The audience will never guess you've forgotten what to say next!

And finally, speak clearly and don't rush. Pretend you're talking to someone who's just learned your language and can best understand you if you enunciate well and don't talk too fast.

It's Debatable

Giving a presentation isn't the only kind of public speaking, of course. There are several others, including the formal debate.

Do you know the difference between a debate and an argument? They have things in common, and they have differences. You can see in this table that various elements are (or should be) constants in a debate but are sometimes true and sometimes not in the less formal argument.

	Debate	Argument
Has two opposing sides or points of view on a subject.	Yes	Yes
The subject is often chosen in advance, allowing participants to prepare their remarks.	Yes	No
Is conducted in a formal, organized manner, with a moderator.	Yes	No
Is often a personal way of fighting with words.	No	Yes
Is either for (pro) or against (con) a specific statement.	Yes	Yes/No
Each side presents information to support their position.	Yes	Yes/No
Each side gives considered, reasonable responses to the other's points.	Yes	Yes/No
Participants are expected to remain calm and courteous.	Yes	Yes/No
The goal is to figure out what is right, not who is right.	Yes	Yes/No
Has a winner officially declared at the end.	Yes	No

Anger Management! --
One of the best ways to *lose* either a debate or an argument is to lose your cool. The moment you get angry, your ability to think clearly and express yourself in a coherent manner goes out the window.

While a formal debate has an established ending, that's often not the case with a personal argument. For that reason, it's essential to know when to call it quits, even when you can't reach an agreement.

When you see that you're never going to persuade the other person to change their mind and are just as certain they're not convincing you to change yours, it's time to agree to disagree, shut it down, and change the subject.

Unresolved arguments that go on and on are destructive to relationships. They produce frustration and anger, which benefits no one.

Mastering the Graceful Exit

Have you ever been in one of those awkward situations where you can't quite wrap up a conversation even though it's clearly over? Even worse than your own feeling of being trapped is when you can tell the other person feels that way too. *Awkward!*

The signs are pretty clear when this is the case. You're bored, and, judging by the body language and facial expression of the other person, you're not alone. You don't need someone yawning in your face to tell you they're feeling the same way you are. Looking down or to the side, forced politeness — these are moments of desperation!

When you've run out of things to say, when either of you starts repeating things, or when sentences turn into phrases such as "Yeah, so" or "Anyway" or nonwords like "uh," "hmm," and "ah," and neither of you goes beyond that, it's time to pull the plug on that conversation.

It's not even as tricky as it often seems! You just need a standard line or two ready. Don't make up an excuse or create a fictitious appointment — that strategy has a way of backfiring on you. Keep it simple. Here are a few suggestions (or create your own):

✓ It was great to see you, but I need to get going.

✓ Glad we had a chance to catch up. You take care!

✓ I've got to run now, sorry! (You might even check the time before saying this.)

That's All, Folks! --
Just remember, whatever you say, make sure it's spoken in an upbeat but firm tone, and then do not hesitate! Give a cheery wave if you like, but *go!* Lingering at that point is just asking for trouble.

It's a little easier to shut down a conversation when you're chatting online, since a word or two is all you need before exiting. A quick "Gotta go" or "Okay, catch you later" will generally suffice. Out of politeness, you should pause just long enough for the other person to post a goodbye of their own.

So Much to Remember!

When we set out to write this book, we wanted it to be as comprehensive and helpful as possible. We hope you've learned things, been surprised at times, and, most of all, begun to experience genuine growth and greater wisdom in the ways you communicate.

You may be wondering, though, how you're ever going to remember all of it!

Don't worry. We won't suddenly materialize in front of you with a pop quiz and shake our heads sadly if you miss an answer.

What we *will* be doing is cheering for you and hoping you make the best possible use of what you've learned ... even though we know very well you've already forgotten some of it.

Yes, it's true. But that's not a problem. Mastering something new doesn't happen overnight. Think of it as a process similar to learning a foreign language or getting the hang of juggling. You can't expect to become proficient on the first attempt. Absorbing and remembering information, practicing, and building new skills — it all takes effort.

And repetition.

Yes, that's right. Reading this book again is a good first step to retaining more of what's inside it. Reading it out loud to yourself — even better! (This is a great tip for studying in general, by the way.) When you read aloud, you are seeing, saying, and hearing the information all at the same time. Engaging yourself while using more than one sense (such as only seeing or only hearing) significantly boosts your recall.

Along the same lines, writing things down — even in point form — is another way to reinforce information. Your hand and brain, working together, will build yet another support for your memory. (And yes, you can add reinforcement by reading what you're writing out loud at the same time — good thinking!) This is why people who make a shopping list are more likely to remember what they intended to purchase even when they forget the list on the table at home!

> **Don't Skip the Activities**
> The best reason not to skip the activities is that they're designed to be fun. But besides that, they get you focused in ways that help make the concepts clearer and easier to remember. Anything designed to reinforce what you've learned is a boost for retention.

And that brings us to what could be your top secret weapon for incredible superpower success.

Practice!

That seems astonishingly obvious, doesn't it? Of course, the more you practice anything, the better you get at it. Anyone who's learned how to play a musical instrument knows how true that is. They also know the importance of making that practice intentional. No one ever became a virtuoso by devoting a little time here and there to their craft. To be effective, practice should become a part of your routine.

That's not to say you have to spend hours every day at it. Just incorporate what you've learned, a little at a time, into your daily routine until it feels completely natural.

You don't need a special place, a designated time, or even a specific goal for practice sessions. Wherever you're comfortable — indoors, outdoors, alone or with others, in front of a mirror, recording yourself to see how you're doing — it's all under your control.

The idea is to work on developing skills so they'll become second nature. Sure, it's a good idea to do a little extra work on areas you know you'll need if you have an important event coming up, but this isn't the kind of thing you learn for a test and forget about afterward. These are skills and facts you'll carry with you and incorporate into your daily life.

You might like to buddy up with someone else in order to practice. It would be really great if you found someone who was just as interested as you are in communication skills superpowers. But anyone who's in your corner and wants to support your efforts will do just fine.

Before you know it, you'll have the confidence you need to handle just about any social situation. And it will show!

That's a Wrap!

Look at you! You've made it to the end of the practical part of this book. (Don't close it just yet, though, we've saved a bunch of fun things for the last chapter.) With all you've discovered and the skills you've acquired, we're betting it's impossible for you to hide your new superpowers. People are noticing, heads are turning, mouths are falling open in astonishment and awe — because, after all, you can't possibly conceal that much cool!

And why should you? Go on out there and dazzle the world!

Chapter Six Activities

Individual Activities

Tame That Temper

Everyone gets angry. Sometimes *really* angry. And when that happens, it's tempting to say things you wouldn't ordinarily say. Mean, insulting things. That might even feel satisfying at the moment, but most people look back on those moments with regret and embarrassment.

The problem is, the offensive words that come rushing out in anger can hurt more than feelings. Damage may be done to reputations, friendships, careers, and more.

There's a way to avoid all of that, if you've prepared ahead of time. Use the following tips so that when those moments of anger come, you'll be ready to respond in ways that are not only inoffensive but may even help defuse the situation.

Creative and Humorous Ways to Express Your Anger

Yes, that's right. Compose some all-purpose responses to use when they're needed. The key is choosing words that express what you want to say but are also, quite frankly, a little amusing. We suggest the following sources — easily found in a search:

✓ Shakespeare, who was a master of the English language. He left behind many marvelous examples of ways to express displeasure without being vulgar.

✓ Other old-fashioned expressions from back in the times when people made something of an art of voicing their frustrations without being rude.

✓ Lists of humorous alternatives to swear words.

Write up a half dozen responses you can memorize so you'll be ready the next time you need to let loose! And don't be surprised if the person on the receiving end looks astonished and maybe even starts to laugh.

Perfect Pitch

Getting used to speaking in public can be challenging, but the more you practice, the easier it will be. Try giving a short talk on one of these ideas (or your own), either in front of a mirror or perhaps with a friend or family member as your audience:

✓ "Why I Call My Pet [Name]." Pets are often given names that tie into their personality, behavior, appearance, and so forth. Choose an imaginary pet — cat, dog, bird, etc. — and give it a funny or unusual name. Then explain what made you select that name for your pet. Have fun with it!

✓ "My Great Invention!" Think of something silly (a shoeshine cloth for the soles of your shoes) or impractical (an underwater candle) and then pretend you're presenting it to a group of billionaires to convince them to give you money to make and sell your product.

✓ "What You Can't See." Select a random photo (from your electronic device or any photo collection) and tell a wild story about what happened right after it was taken.

✓ "Changing Lanes." We've all been in conversations where someone wanders from subject to subject. Try giving a full, one-minute talk doing exactly that — bouncing around from topic to topic. Switch from happy to sad, funny, upsetting, and so on, so that you're changing your tone, expression, and body language to fit each new subject.

Group Activities

Two Sides!

This activity will help you learn how to sharpen your skills for debates or even disagreements!

First, select topics for the activity. Samples are shown below, but you can find many others online or write up your own.

Break into an even number of small groups.

Each group is to make lists of *both* the pros and cons related to the topic.

Discuss how participants' personal opinions influence them in creating support for each side of the debate. Discuss how considering both sides of the subject can help with strategy and persuasive arguments.

Sample Subjects:

✓ Is a hamburger a sandwich?

✓ Should you lend money to a close friend?

✓ Is it right to keep wild animals in a zoo?

✓ Should people in prison be allowed to vote?

✓ Should everyone's DNA be stored in a national database?

The Best of Me

Being confident is hugely important for anyone learning new skills. But it's not always easy to give ourselves the pats on the back that we deserve. Often, it feels more natural to compliment someone else than it is to acknowledge our own qualities, skills, and achievements.

For this activity, participants are going to list the top three things they like about each of the others on a sheet of paper, with at least one of the items being related to communication. For example: how empathetic they are, the way they analyze information, their use of body language, the way they speak, their listening skills, and so on.

Allow enough space between each name so that the pages can be divided later.

Once completed, the pages will be turned in to an adult group leader. The leader will then cut the pages to separate the names, and each person will be given the slips that are about them.

Being aware of the qualities others see in you can be a powerful confidence booster. Save those slips and review them whenever you need a little encouragement.

Chapter Six Rapid Recap

✓ Restrict the use of a potty mouth to casual conversations with like-minded friends.

✓ Remember that nervousness about public speaking is common and can be overcome with preparation and practice.

✓ Seeing both sides of an issue can not only improve debating skills but also help you keep an open mind.

✓ Exit a conversation gracefully and politely.

✓ Practicing good conversation skills will have far-reaching benefits in your social life and, later on, in your professional life.

-CHAPTER SEVEN-

Let's Talk

Now that you've achieved superpower status in communication, what should you talk about? How about — anything you like! There are literally millions of subjects, thoughts, and ideas just waiting to be explored.

Common interests are a great starting point when you're first getting to know someone, but figuring out what those interests are can take a little exploration.

Imagine yourself at a social event, and you've just been introduced to a stranger. You exchange a few words and then find yourself trapped in an awkward patch of silence. Your first urge will likely be to mumble an excuse and move on. Well, don't do it! You could be missing an opportunity to get to know someone who could become a close friend, a person of real importance in your life.

So, no! Don't skitter off! Have some topics tucked away in your noggin, ready to help you kick-start a genuine conversation.

Conversation Starters

We've put together some sample questions that you might find useful when you'd like to turn awkward moments of dead air into vibrant conversations.

But don't limit yourself to this list; we know you can come up with plenty of others that fit your personal interests.

One tip: avoid too many questions that can be answered with "Yes" or "No." Instead, try to pose those that are likely to spark some genuine discussion.

✓ What do you like to do in your spare time?

✓ Tell me your favorite song from the last year.

✓ What's your top pick in fast foods?

✓ What kind of sports are you into?

✓ Do you have any specific plans for the future?

✓ What other places have you lived?

✓ Which social media platforms do you use?

✓ What's the best movie you've ever seen?

✓ What do you think was the greatest invention of the last decade?

✓ Which time of year do you like the best?

✓ What kind of animal do you think makes the best pet?

✓ Do you take your phone with you everywhere you go?

✓ Are there any foods you refuse to try?

✓ If you could meet someone famous, who would you pick?

✓ Do you have any pet peeves?

✓ What does your family usually do on vacation?

✓ What's the best book you've ever read?

✓ Do you have any phobias?

✓ Do you think everyone should do some kind of volunteer work?

✓ Are you a binge-watcher when you find a new show you like?

✓ What's the best song to listen to when you want to pick yourself up?

Reflection and Exploration: Things to Discuss

You will be surprised what you can learn about yourself and others when you encounter questions that require a bit of reflection. Values, principles, ideals, hopes, dreams, and so much more will rise to the surface as you explore and discuss questions such as those in the following collection. And don't be afraid to come up with some of your own as well!

Here is a sampling of what we hope you'll find to be fun and interesting things to discuss with friends, family, and others:

✓ What is your most prized possession and why?

✓ Imagine that for one full year you can only speak the truth. How would that affect you and those around you?

✓ If you could ask any one question and be guaranteed you would be given the true answer to it, what would your question be?

✓ Is there a movie you've watched so many times you know parts by heart? What makes it so special?

Ideas come in all shapes and sizes!

✓ Would it be a good or a bad thing if all the world's wealth were evenly distributed?

✓ Does stealing harm the thief?

✓ Has there ever been a word/phrase fad that you came to despise?

✓ Is envy always a bad thing?

✓ Think of something you're afraid to do. What would it take for you to do it in spite of your fear?

✓ What is the number one thing that makes you lose track of time?

✓ Should motive be taken into account when deciding the punishment for a crime?

✓ Is there something you would like to learn how to do? If so, is anything standing in your way?

✓ Which one of these three senses would you give up if you had to choose: sight, hearing, or taste?

✓ Is it harder to forgive yourself for harming someone else or to forgive someone else for harming you?

✓ Is it ever right to do the wrong thing?

✓ If you could see one specific life event in the future, what would you choose?

✓ Is peace more likely if everyone is armed or if no one is?

✓ What are the best and worst reasons for a person to be admired?

✓ Is theft from a person worse than theft from a company?

✓ What is the most important factor in determining a person's value?

✓ Would you rather be incredibly rich or incredibly smart?

✓ What are the two most important qualities in an ideal life partner?

✓ What is the most vital thing in a friendship?

✓ What one superpower would you choose if you could?

✓ When is silence more meaningful than words?

✓ Is it ever wrong to do the right thing?

✓ What message would you like to send yourself at some time in your past?

✓ What type of crime would you be most likely to commit if you knew you would never be caught?

✓ If you could alter one single thing in your genes, what would it be?

✓ If given the option, would you want to know the date on which you are going to die?

✓ Do we judge others on their actions but judge ourselves by our intentions?

✓ What's the most outrageous trick you've ever fallen for?

✓ What is your favorite way to justify an unnecessary purchase?

✓ What book would you like to make mandatory for everyone to read?

✓ If you had a chance to go to the moon, would you?

✓ Which of your ancestors would you most like to know more about?

✓ What fashion style did you love at the time but shudder thinking about now?

✓ If you could be invisible for a day, how would you spend your time?

✓ What would you most like to be remembered for?

✓ If you had to give up one of your favorite foods forever, what would it be?

✓ What's the longest stretch of time you've ever spent watching television in one sitting?

✓ Are there any words you've said incorrectly as a small child that you or your family still mispronounce?

✓ Is there anything you'd like to learn to do if you had more free time?

Creative Exploration Activity — Where Did THAT Come From?

There are some very interesting expressions, known as idioms, in the English language. How many are you familiar with? And what do you think they really mean?

Have you ever stopped to wonder where some of those idioms first came from?

Have fun guessing how some of the following expressions got started, and be sure to see if you can find out the actual history of each expression when you're done.

✓ Every cloud has a silver lining.

✓ That's a horse of a different color.

✓ Give someone the cold shoulder.

✓ Birds of a feather flock together.

✓ Wet your whistle.

✓ Don't give up your day job.

✓ That's the pot calling the kettle black.

✓ It's raining cats and dogs.

✓ He's barking up the wrong tree.

✓ Don't spill the beans.

✓ To escape by the skin of your teeth.

✓ Someone who's on the ball.

✓ Like closing the barn door after the horse has bolted.

✓ A taste of your own medicine.

✓ Don't put all your eggs in one basket.

✓ Make hay while the sun shines.

✓ It's a piece of cake.

✓ Don't cut corners.

✓ The ball is in your court.

✓ A wild goose chase.

✓ Bite the bullet.

✓ You're up the creek without a paddle.

✓ There's a frog in my throat.

✓ To let the cat out of the bag.

✓ We missed the boat.

✓ Break a leg.

✓ Killing two birds with one stone.

✓ Don't burn your bridges.

✓ He kicked the bucket.

✓ Run like the wind.

Add other expressions you've heard to the list!

-ACKNOWLEDGMENTS-

Our heartfelt thanks to Barry Jowett for his support and editing skills through all stages of this project.

Thanks also to Marijke Friesen for her fabulous work on the design.

The entire Cormorant/DCB team is consistently wonderful to work with and we appreciate all their efforts.

We are especially honored that *More than Words* was chosen as the debut nonfiction title to be published by DCB Young Readers.

Valerie also thanks her co-creators, Natalie and David. There appeared to be no limit to Natalie's patience, or her willingness to share her expertise with this NF novice. David, as usual, produced artwork that fit the project so very well, all without complaining (that we know of) about our requests for "wee" changes. And as always, Valerie thanks her husband, Brent, for his unwavering encouragement.

Natalie hopes her body language, word choices, and responses indicated to her co-creators, Valerie and David, how much she enjoyed working with both of them. She also wants to thank her husband, Craig, and her children for all the communication and debate skills she had the opportunity to practice over the years trying to decipher their messages.

David also thanks his co-creators, Valerie and Natalie, for their bottomless pit of patience. He also wants to thank his wife, Geraldine, and his children, Lorne and Alice, for their constant support during this project.

The Language of Communication

accent a distinctive pronunciation of words common to one area of the world

argue give an opposing view

articulate express an idea clearly

body language gestures and expressions that contribute to the meaning of a message

communicate share information, news, or ideas

conversation a talk between two or more people

converse to participate in a conversation

delivery the style and tone in which you speak to someone

dialogue back-and-forth conversation between two or more people

/137

discourse written or spoken communication

empathy the ability to understand and share the feeling of
someone else

enunciate say or pronounce very clearly

eye contact looking directly into someone else's eyes

facial expression movements created by parts of the face to
express emotions

gossip conversation about other people, often including details
not proven to be true

interrupt to break into a conversation

nonverbal not using spoken words

passive-aggressive indirectly expressing anger

pronounce make the sound of letters or words in the correct way

tone of voice how you sound when you say words out loud

verbal using spoken words

vocalize say out loud

volume how loud something sounds

Natalie Hyde is the author of both fiction and non-fiction for middle-grade and young adult readers. Her works include *Saving Armpit*, *Up the Creek*, and *Swept Away*, and her books have received award nominations in both Canada and the US including the Rocky Mountain, Silver Birch, and Nutmeg Awards. She currently lives in Flamborough, Ontario.

Valerie Sherrard is an award-winning author of picture books and middle-grade and young adult novels. Her novel *The Glory Wind* won the Geoffrey Bilson and the Ann Connor Brimer Awards. Her works have been chosen as Silver Birch and Red Maple Award Honour Books, and garnered other readers' choice award nominations including the MYRCA, the Hackmatack, and the Saskatchewan Willows. Born in Moose Jaw, Saskatchewan, she now lives in Miramichi, New Brunswick.

David Jardine is an illustrator and YouTuber whose video series "Coffee Doodles" has been showcased on major news sites like Yahoo News and MSN. Jardine's work has been nominated for the Forest of Reading Blue Spruce Award and Saskatchewan's Willow Award. His work has been exhibited at the Harbourfront Gallery, Rodman Hall Gallery, and the Sean O'Sullivan Theatre Gallery. He lives in Miramichi, New Brunswick. For more information on David, please visit davidjardineart.com.

We acknowledge the sacred land on which Cormorant Books operates. It has been a site of human activity for 15,000 years. This land is the territory of the Huron-Wendat and Petun First Nations, the Seneca, and most recently, the Mississaugas of the Credit River. The territory was the subject of the Dish With One Spoon Wampum Belt Covenant, an agreement between the Iroquois Confederacy and Confederacy of the Ojibway and allied nations to peaceably share and steward the resources around the Great Lakes. Today, the meeting place of Toronto is still home to many Indigenous people from across Turtle Island. We are grateful to have the opportunity to work in the community, on this territory.

We are also mindful of broken covenants and the need to strive to make right with all our relations.